Generis
PUBLISHING

Network Hypothesis of Consciousness

B.A. Lobasyuk

Title: **Network Hypothesis of Consciousness**

ISBN: 979-8-89966-452-6

Author: B.A. Lobasyuk

Cover image: www.pixabay.com

Publisher: Generis Publishing
Online orders: www.generis-publishing.com
Contact email: info@generis-publishing.com

Lobasyuk B.A.

Network Hypothesis of Consciousness

Consciousness in Animals: Neurophysiological, Cognitive, and Philosophical Foundations

Cognitive Manifestations and Experimental Tests of Consciousness in Animals

Emotional and Affective Consciousness in Animals

Comparative Analysis of Human and Animal Consciousness

Human Consciousness: Neurophysiological, Cognitive, and Comparative Aspects

The Unconscious in Sigmund Freud's Theory

Neofreudianism

The Network Semantic-Topological Model of Consciousness by B.A. Lobasyuk

The Psyche as a Network of Meanings and Topologies

Fundamental Principles of the Network Semantic-Topological Method

2026

ABSTRACT

The research provides a comprehensive interdisciplinary study of consciousness and the unconscious in animals and humans within neurophysiological, cognitive, philosophical, and evolutionary frameworks. It explores the evolutionary foundations of consciousness, neural correlates of awareness, and cognitive and emotional manifestations of mental activity. Special attention is given to the comparison between animal and human forms of consciousness, as well as to the analysis of the unconscious — from Freud's psychoanalytic concept to modern network and cognitive models. The study proposes an **integrative network semantic-topological model of consciousness**, combining psychoanalytic, cognitive, and neurophysiological approaches, and demonstrates a shift from classical dualistic concepts to a systemic, network, and evolutionary understanding of the psyche.

Keywords: consciousness; unconscious; neural correlates; cognitive processes; evolution of the psyche; network model of consciousness; psychoanalysis; neurophilosophy.

TABLE OF CONTENTS

1. Animal Consciousness: Neurophysiological, Cognitive, and Philosophical Foundations

The question of consciousness in animals occupies a special place among the fundamental issues of modern brain science. It lies at the intersection of neurophysiology, cognitive psychology, ethology, and philosophy of mind. Already in the first half of the 20th century, physiologists and psychologists—I.M. Sechenov, I.P. Pavlov, and N.A. Bernstein—noted that animal behavior cannot be reduced to a simple reflex chain: it includes internal models of the external world, anticipation of the outcomes of actions, and selective attention to significant stimuli.

Within the framework of the domestic school of systems physiology, P.K. Anokhin (1975) developed the concept of a functional system—a dynamic organization that includes not only effector, but also afferent, integrative, and evaluative components. In this model, the emergence of consciousness is associated with the appearance of afferent synthesis and a "feedback-from-result" mechanism, which forms the subjective experience of correspondence between action and goal. Later, B.A. Lobasyuk (2010, 2023) demonstrated that the systemic organization of brain electric activity and interhemispheric interactions create neuronal prerequisites for cognitive integration, which can be considered a neurophysiological prototype of consciousness.

Contemporary international science develops similar ideas, relying on models of information integration and global neural networks (Dehaene & Naccache, 2001; Tononi, 2008). Consciousness is viewed as the result of coordinated activity of multiple distributed ensembles that unite sensory, motor, and limbic systems. In this context, the question of animal consciousness acquires not only a philosophical but also a strictly empirical dimension: is it possible to detect in animal brains mechanisms equivalent to human neural correlates of conscious experience?

From an evolutionary and functional perspective, consciousness does not emerge suddenly but develops gradually as a complication of systems for self-regulation, orientation, and social interaction (Merker, 2007; Panksepp, 2011). Neurophysiological organization supporting attention, emotional evaluation, and prediction of action outcomes is observed in many species—from fish and birds to mammals. In this sense, one can speak of a continuum of awareness, where different animals occupy different levels depending on the complexity of neural networks, brain architecture, and social-cognitive environment (Birch et al., 2020).

Research over recent decades has shown that many animals demonstrate behaviors reflecting elements of self-reference and metacognitive evaluation. Successful performance in the mirror test by dolphins (Reiss & Marino, 2001), elephants (Plotnik et al., 2006), and corvids (Prior et al., 2008) indicates the presence of a basic level of self-awareness. More complex manifestations of cognitive consciousness—such as metacognition, planning, and deferred problem solving—are observed in great apes (Smith et al., 2003; Call & Tomasello, 2008).

Thus, the question of animal consciousness ceases to be purely philosophical: it acquires concrete neurophysiological content. The task of science is to identify the precise mechanisms—rhythmic, neural-network, limbic—that enable the formation of subjective experience in animals.

2. Evolutionary Preconditions and Neurophysiological Correlates of Consciousness

2.1. Evolution of Integrative Brain Mechanisms

Consciousness, like other cognitive functions, does not appear suddenly but evolves based on the complication of sensory integration and behavioral regulation mechanisms. According to Anokhin's classical concept (1975), the basis of any mental activity is a functional system in which the outcome of an action is evaluated against the expected result. This mechanism of afferent synthesis and feedback from results can be considered a physiological precursor of subjective evaluation, i.e., a primary analog of conscious states.

From the perspective of neurophysiological evolution, the most important prerequisites for the formation of consciousness were the emergence of structures ensuring:

Multichannel sensory integration (thalamus, diencephalon)

Emotional evaluation of stimuli (limbic system)

Anticipation and behavioral correction (frontal and prefrontal areas in higher mammals)

Comparative neuroanatomy studies show that in vertebrates there is a gradual differentiation of structures performing integration and behavioral modulation functions (Butler & Hodos, 2005). In fish and amphibians, this role is played by the midbrain and reticular formation; in birds, by the hyperpallium, which performs functions homologous to the mammalian neocortex (Güntürkün, 2012). Thus, the evolution of consciousness is the evolution of integration networks capable of internal environmental modeling.

B.A. Lobasyuk (2010, 2023) demonstrated that brain electric activity, realized in networks of cortical and subcortical structures, represents not merely a sum of bioelectrical processes, but a systemic organization in which each rhythm carries a specific integrative function. According to him, interhemispheric asymmetry, variability of frequency–amplitude correlations, and the presence of intersystem connections create the basis for phenomenal unity of perception—a counterpart to the wholeness of consciousness.

In this sense, consciousness can be viewed as having evolved as a form of optimization of energy and information processes in the brain (Lobasyuk, 2010), ensuring maximal efficiency in selecting behavioral strategies.

2.2. From Reflex to Neural Model of the World

The transition from simple reflex systems to cognitive forms of behavior was accompanied by the development of the ability to internally model the environment. This idea was first expressed by I.M. Sechenov (1863) and I.P. Pavlov (1928), who emphasized that the brain does not simply react to stimuli, but constructs temporal links and predictions.

In the 20th century, N.A. Bernstein (1947) developed the concept of anticipatory reflection, noting that animal behavior is formed based on the active construction of an action program. These principles were later neurophysiologically confirmed: experiments in primates identified neurons that activate in anticipation of action outcomes, even in the absence of movement (Rizzolatti & Craighero, 2004). These predictive neurons, part of the mirror neuron system, are considered the basis of empathy and social consciousness.

From the standpoint of systems neurophysiology (Anokhin, 1975; Sudakov, 1993), the ability to anticipate is a key criterion of consciousness because it implies an internal representation of possible outcomes. In animals, this manifests as the ability to plan routes, assess the probability of success, and adjust actions based on external feedback.

Thus, evolutionarily, consciousness grows out of the mechanism of feedback from results, acquiring the character of a neural model of the external world, maintained by reverberation of activity in cortico-subcortical networks (Edelman, 2004).

2.3. Neural Networks and Synchronization as the Basis of Awareness

Modern research in network neurophysiology shows that conscious perception is associated not with localized activation of individual centers, but with global synchronization of neuronal activity in the beta- and gamma-frequency ranges (Dehaene & Changeux, 2011; Tononi, 2008). These rhythms serve as a universal mechanism for uniting heterogeneous sensory and cognitive processes into a single temporal structure—what Edelman (2004) called reentrant integration.

Studies by B.A. Lobasyuk and colleagues (Lobasyuk B.A., Bartsevich L.B., Zamkova A.V., 2023) within the framework of a network semantic-topological model of brain electric activity showed that the structure of intersystem EEG rhythm correlations reflects the degree of functional integration corresponding to the state of cognitive activity. In particular, in mammals solving tasks of varying complexity, interhemispheric synchronization in the alpha and beta ranges increases—a marker of coordination between local and global networks.

This aligns with the global neuronal workspace concept (Baars, 2002; Dehaene & Naccache, 2001), according to which consciousness arises when information spreads throughout the cognitive network and becomes "available" to multiple brain systems.

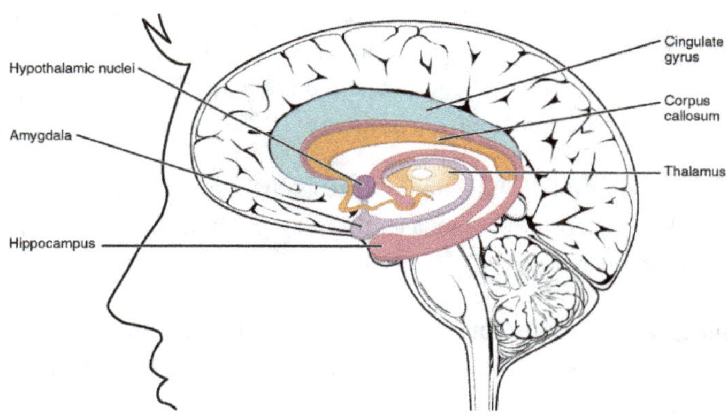

Figure 1. Limbic System

The limbic system, particularly the cingulate cortex and amygdala, provides the emotional coloring of perception, creating the phenomenological aspect of consciousness—subjective experience of the significance of stimuli (Panksepp, 2011). Thus, two levels of neural organization of consciousness can be distinguished:

1. **Sensorimotor level** – synchronization of networks integrating perception and action.
2. **Affective-evaluative level** – involvement of limbic structures that form the subjective significance of events.

The joint functioning of these levels gives rise to what can be called **primary consciousness** (Edelman, 2004)—awareness of events in the present moment without abstract reflection.

2.4. Neurophysiological Criteria for the Presence of Consciousness in Animals

Comparison of neurophysiological data, behavioral experiments, and brain structure analysis allows us to identify a set of criteria by which elementary forms of consciousness in animals can be inferred:

1. Presence of thalamocortical loops ensuring the integration of sensory signals (Edelman & Seth, 2009).
2. Synchronization of cortical networks in the gamma range during perception of novel stimuli (Dehaene & Changeux, 2011).
3. Activation of the cingulate gyrus and medial frontal areas during choice between alternatives (Mashour et al., 2020).
4. Detection of responses analogous to the human P300 component during conscious stimulus discrimination (Seth, 2018).
5. Behavioral signs of self-reference and metacognition indicating the presence of internal information control (Smith et al., 2003).

Integration of these indicators suggests that animal consciousness has objective neurophysiological correlates, measurable using EEG, neuroimaging, and functional connectivity analysis.

Thus, animal consciousness can be described as a dynamic network of coordinated brain states, providing internal coherence of perception and behavioral action.

3. Evolutionary Preconditions of Animal Consciousness

Animal consciousness should not be considered a property that arises suddenly; it is the product of the long-term evolution of the nervous system, aimed at increasing behavioral adaptability and efficiency. The evolutionary approach to consciousness dates back to Charles Darwin, who argued that the differences between human and animal minds are quantitative rather than qualitative (Darwin, 1871). This position was later developed in comparative psychology and cognitive ethology, where consciousness is viewed as a **continuum**—from elementary forms of sensory integration to reflective awareness (Griffin, 1984; Shettleworth, 2010).

3.1. From Reflex to Integrative Forms of Mental Activity

The earliest neural forms of information processing appeared in multicellular animals at the level of network structures (Cnidaria, Echinodermata), where specialized brain centers did not yet exist. These structures performed integration and movement coordination functions—precursors of future neural ensembles (Edelman, 1992).

In invertebrates, rudimentary forms of "internal state" can already be observed—for example, changes in responsiveness depending on past experience or context. A classic example is learning in *Aplysia* (Kandel, 2001), where simple neural networks demonstrate elementary memory and modification of responses. While such processes are not conscious in the human sense, they represent an important transitional stage from purely sensorimotor schemes to cognitive modules.

In the Russian physiological tradition, I.M. Sechenov (1863) and I.P. Pavlov (1903) emphasized that a reflex is not an automatic response but a dynamic system modified by experience and environment. This idea effectively anticipated P.K. Anokhin's concept of **functional systems** (1975), in which behavior is seen as the result of interactions between multiple levels of neural regulation aimed at achieving a useful outcome. In the context of consciousness evolution, this theory is particularly valuable: it shows that subjective experience is the product of systemic integration, not a single center.

3.2. Limbic Evolution and the Emergence of Emotional Consciousness

With the emergence of vertebrates, a qualitative leap occurred: structures of the limbic system, especially the hippocampus and amygdala, formed, creating prerequisites for emotional and motivational behavior. Emotions became internal signals regulating behavior and enabling the animal to predict the significance of events (Panksepp, 1998).

According to J. Panksepp, basic emotional systems such as **SEEKING, FEAR, RAGE, CARE, LUST, PLAY, PANIC** can already be identified in mammals, each associated with specific neurochemical and neuroanatomical circuits (Panksepp & Biven, 2012). These systems not only regulate behavior but also create the phenomenological basis of conscious experience—the "affective core" of subjectivity.

Ukrainian and Russian studies (Lobasyuk, 2010; Sudakov, 1997; Sokolov, 2002) emphasize that emotional reactions in animals have a network character and are formed through interstructural interactions between limbic-reticular and cortical levels. The transition from automatic emotional responses to cognitively modulated states is a key mechanism in the formation of consciousness.

3.3. Neocortex Development and Cognitive Integration

With the evolution of the neocortex in higher mammals (especially primates and dolphins), a fundamental reorganization of brain architecture occurred: connections between sensory, motor, and associative zones were strengthened. This enabled the formation of **metarepresentations**—"representations of representations" (Dehaene & Changeux, 2011). These structures provide a **working space for consciousness**, integrating heterogeneous sensory and cognitive information.

EEG and fMRI studies have shown that in primates and some birds (corvids, parrots), neural networks analogous to human consciousness networks—anterior cingulate cortex, insula, thalamus—are activated (Mashour et al., 2020). This indicates that animals possess not only reactive but also reflective forms of mental activity.

Thus, the evolution of consciousness in animals is a gradual process of integrating sensory, motor, emotional, and cognitive systems into a unified neural network capable of internally modeling the world and the self within it.

4. Neurophysiological Correlates of Consciousness in Animals

Understanding the neurophysiological basis of consciousness in animals requires analysis of the structures and mechanisms that support information integration, attention, perception, emotional evaluation, and behavioral choice. Modern neuroscience views consciousness not as a localized function but as a **network property of the brain**, emerging from the interaction of distributed ensembles of neurons (Edelman & Tononi, 2000; Dehaene, 2014; Lobasyuk, 2023).

4.1. Thalamocortical System and Global Integration

One of the key candidates for the neural basis of consciousness is the **thalamocortical loop**—an interconnected network including the specific and nonspecific thalamic nuclei, the reticular formation, and cortical associative areas (Llinás, 2001). This system enables the **global binding of sensory signals into a unified cognitive representation**, making the emergence of subjective experience possible.

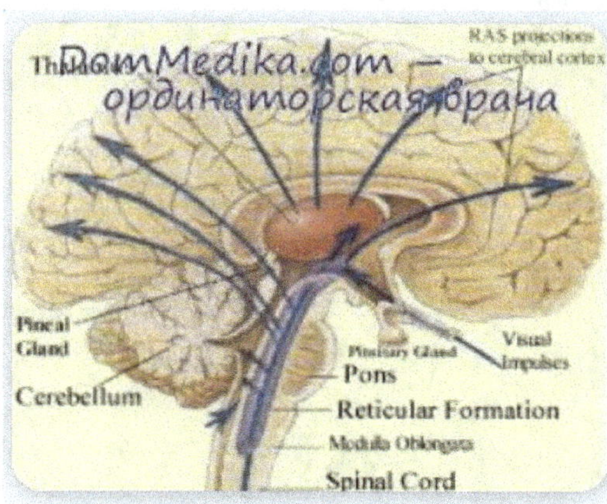

Figure 2. Thalamocortical System

Animal studies have shown that **correlates of conscious states** (e.g., wakefulness, orienting responses, exploration) are accompanied by **high-frequency neuronal synchronization** (30–80 Hz) between the thalamus and the cortex (Steriade, 1996; Gaillard et al., 2009). This **γ-synchronization** ensures coordination between distributed brain regions and is considered the physiological substrate of the "unity of perception."

Domestic studies (Lobasyuk, 2010; Lobasyuk, Bartsevich & Zamkova, 2023) demonstrated that functional states of the brain are characterized by **dynamic reorganizations of the network structure** of cortico-subcortical interactions. Lobasyuk (2023) proposed a **network semantic-topological model of brain electrical activity**, in which consciousness is viewed as a process of **self-consistency among neuronal ensemble activities**, reflecting the holistic organization of the system. Within this model, **coherence of rhythms** (particularly in the α- and β-bands) serves as an index of **integrative processes** closely associated with the phenomenology of the conscious act.

4.2. Reticular Formation and the Activation System

The **reticular formation of the brainstem** has traditionally been considered the physiological basis of **wakefulness and attention** (Moruzzi & Magoun, 1949). It regulates the **excitability of the cortex**, thereby creating the conditions necessary for the emergence of conscious states. In animals, suppression of reticular formation activity induces **coma-like or sleep-like states**, while electrical stimulation restores **orienting responses and exploratory activity**.

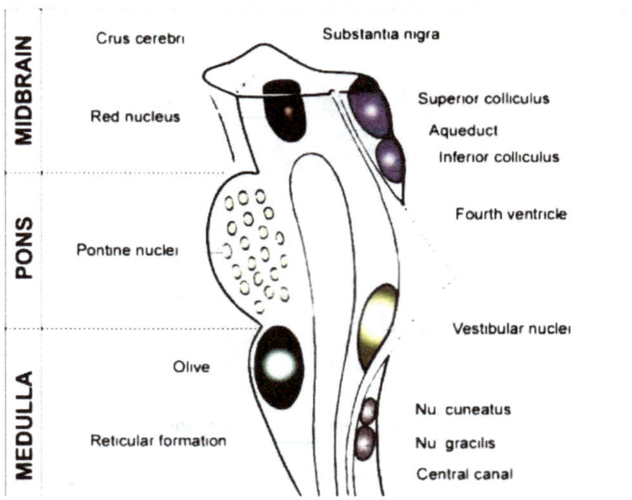

Figure 3. Pontomedullary Reticular Formation

Recent data clarify that the activation system is not merely a "switch" for consciousness, but a hierarchically organized network that includes cholinergic, noradrenergic, and serotonergic pathways which modulate cognitive and emotional processes (Jones, 2003). Experiments on cats and rats have shown that the transition from sleep to wakefulness is accompanied by an increase in γ-rhythm coherence between the cortex and hippocampus (Vanderwolf, 2000).

Studies by Ukrainian neurophysiologists (Lobasyuk, 2023) confirm that the rhythmic organization of the bioelectrical activity of the animal brain is a universal mechanism that ensures the network integration of structures into a single functional system. In this interpretation, consciousness is the result of internal synchronization and self-organization of neural networks.

4.3. Neural Correlates of Consciousness (NCC) in Animals

The term *neural correlates of consciousness* (NCC), introduced by F. Crick and C. Koch (Crick & Koch, 1990), refers to the minimal neural mechanisms sufficient for the emergence of subjective experience. Although we cannot directly assess subjectivity in animals, behavioral and neurophysiological indicators make it possible to identify states functionally equivalent to conscious ones.

In monkeys, dolphins, and corvid birds, patterns of neural activity have been identified that are analogous to those in humans during cognitive tasks requiring conscious choice. For example, in metacognition tests, activation occurs in prefrontal and cingulate regions associated with self-reference (Kornell et al., 2007; Clayton & Emery, 2015).

Of particular significance is the spontaneous cortical activity observed in some animals during rest and sleep — it forms the so-called *default mode network* (DMN), analogous to the human resting-state network (Buckner et al., 2008). This indicates the presence of an internal model of the world in animals and, possibly, of self-aware planning.

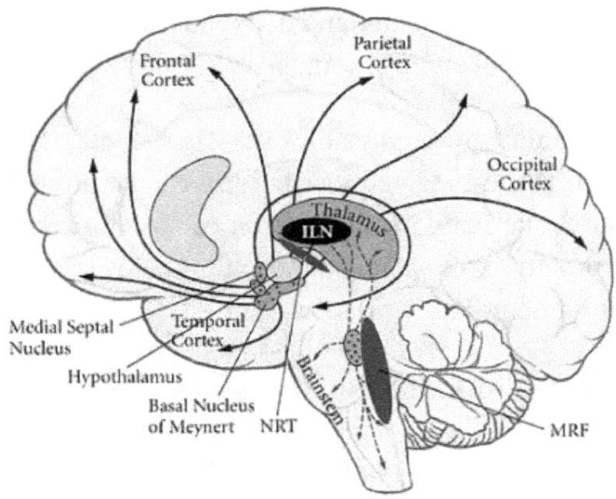

Figure 4. *Midline structures in the brainstem and thalamus are essential for regulating the level of cortical arousal. Small bilateral lesions in many of these nuclei cause a global loss of consciousness.*

4.4. Network Neurophysiology and the Dynamics of Integrative Rhythms

Modern studies of consciousness increasingly rely on network-based analytical methods — correlation, topological, and information-theoretic models (Friston, 2011; B. A. Lobasyuk et al., 2025). These approaches demonstrate that a key prerequisite for a conscious state is an optimal level of neural network connectivity — a balance between excessive synchrony (rigidity, as in epilepsy) and chaotic desynchronization (loss of perceptual unity).

Lobasyuk and colleagues (2019, 2021) showed that interhemispheric asymmetry coefficients and rhythm coherence indices reflect the degree of integration of the brain's functional systems. Changes in these parameters under pharmacological influences (for example, thyroliberin or polyphenolic factors) reveal the plasticity of network organization associated with cognitive and emotional processes.

Thus, findings from network neurophysiology confirm that consciousness in animals is not an abstract property but a real network state, characterized by a balance of connectivity, asymmetry, and rhythmic coordination.

5. COGNITIVE MANIFESTATIONS AND EXPERIMENTAL TESTS OF CONSCIOUSNESS IN ANIMALS

The study of consciousness in animals is inevitably tied to the problem of operationalization: how can we determine whether an animal possesses subjective experience if it cannot verbalize it? Contemporary cognitive ethology and neuropsychology propose a range of behavioral and neurophysiological tests designed to detect signs of self-reference, anticipation, metacognition, and goal awareness (Griffin, 1984; Shettleworth, 2010; De Waal, 2016).

5.1. The Mirror Recognition Test

One of the most well-known criteria for self-awareness is the *mirror test* proposed by G. G. Gallup (1970). The essence of the method is to place a mark on the animal's body that is visible only in a mirror. If the animal uses the reflection to inspect or remove the mark, this is interpreted as evidence of visual self-recognition.

The mirror test has been successfully passed by:

- Great apes (chimpanzees, orangutans, bonobos);
- Dolphins (Reiss & Marino, 2001);
- Asian elephants (Plotnik et al., 2006);
- Certain bird species (magpies, Prior et al., 2008).

However, failure to pass the mirror test does not imply the absence of consciousness. Dogs and corvids, for instance, exhibit other forms of self-awareness — olfactory and social. Behavioral observations show that these animals can recognize themselves by scent (Horowitz, 2017) or by the contextual roles they play in social interactions, which requires a cognitive model of the "self" as an agent of *action.

Figure 5. Mirror Recognition Test

It is believed that mirror recognition represents only an external behavioral index, while the neurophysiological essence of self-awareness lies in the network self-organization of brain activity that enables internal reflection. In experiments with interhemispheric models, Lobasyuk (2022) demonstrated that the balance between asymmetry and rhythm synchronization corresponds to the degree of internal self-control and cognitive coordination of actions.

5.2. Metamemory and Awareness of Knowledge

Another indicator of consciousness is *metamemory* — the ability to know that one knows or does not know. This form of metacognition has been identified in several animal species, including dolphins (Smith et al., 1995), macaques (Hampton, 2001), and crows (Watanabe & Clayton, 2016).

Classic experiments show that animals can refuse to perform a task when uncertain of the correct answer, or seek additional information before making a decision. This suggests the presence of reflective evaluation of internal states — a cognitive predicate of consciousness.

fMRI studies in primates have shown that during such tasks, activation occurs in the anterior cingulate cortex and dorsolateral prefrontal areas — regions analogous to those involved in conscious control in humans (Kornell et al., 2007). Thus, animal metamemory reflects elementary forms of self-referential processing.

5.3. Theory of Mind

Theory of Mind (ToM) refers to the ability to attribute mental states — intentions, beliefs, emotions — to other beings. The first experiments, conducted by Premack and Woodruff (1978), demonstrated that chimpanzees can understand the purpose of human actions.

Subsequent studies (Call & Tomasello, 2008; Bugnyar, 2011) have shown that crows and dolphins display the ability to take another's perspective and predict their behavior. For example, crows hide food differently when they know they are being observed — and relocate it once the observer leaves.

Such behavior cannot be explained by simple conditioning; it requires a model of another's mental state, implying the presence of rudimentary *secondary consciousness* (Dennett, 1991).

In the context of network neurophysiology (Lobasyuk, 2023, 2025), this ability can be interpreted as a *cognitive simulation* of another's state based on an internal model. Such simulation requires activation of distributed networks in parietal, prefrontal, and limbic regions — structures responsible for "subject modeling."

5.4. Planning and Goal-Directed Behavior

Many animals exhibit the ability to plan actions that extend beyond immediate motivation. A classic example is the behavior of crows, which can select a tool suitable for a future task even when the reward will be obtained later (Raby et al., 2007). Similar forms of "deferred planning" have been observed in primates (Mulcahy & Call, 2006).

Such behavior implies the existence of a *temporal model of consciousness*, allowing the animal to represent the future and act in the present with it in mind. This function relies on hippocampal–prefrontal circuits responsible for the temporal organization of experience (Clayton et al., 2003).

During planning tasks, animals show changes in interhemispheric asymmetry coefficients of α-rhythms, indicating a redistribution of activity between hemispheres during cognitive forecasting. This supports the hypothesis that the temporal structure of consciousness arises from the dynamic interaction of interhemispheric and network processes.

5.5. Tool Use and Conceptual Categorization

The ability to use tools is considered an important indicator of cognitive consciousness. Tool use and even tool creation have been documented in chimpanzees, crows, dolphins, and otters (Boesch & Tomasello, 1998; Emery & Clayton, 2004).

This suggests that the animal can distinguish means from ends and therefore possesses a representational model of action. Neurophysiologically, this process is based on *mirror neurons* — discovered by Rizzolatti (Rizzolatti & Sinigaglia, 2010) — which are activated both during the execution and observation of an action. These neurons provide the foundation for imitative learning and empathy, key components of conscious interaction.

Within the network framework (Lobasyuk, 2025), tool use is interpreted as a manifestation of *semantic integration* — the ability to link neural representations of objects and actions into a unified semantic circuit. This represents one of the neurophysiological criteria of conscious thought.

Figure 6. *Chimpanzee Raphael in I. P. Pavlov's experiments using a pole to move from one raft to another.*

6. EMOTIONAL AND AFFECTIVE CONSCIOUSNESS IN ANIMALS

Emotions are an integral part of consciousness and its phenomenological dimension. They provide the evaluative coloration of experience, guide behavior, and form internal motives for action. Understanding emotional consciousness in animals requires the integration of data from neurophysiology, behavioral experiments, and cognitive theory.

6.1. Basic Emotional Systems and Their Neurophysiological Correlates

Jaak Panksepp (Panksepp, 1998; Panksepp & Biven, 2012) identified seven primary emotional systems present in mammals: **SEEKING** (exploration, curiosity), **FEAR**, **RAGE** (anger/aggression), **CARE** (nurturing), **LUST** (reproductive motivation), **PLAY**, and **PANIC/GRIEF** (separation distress and sadness).

Each system has distinct neurochemical and anatomical circuits involving the limbic system, hypothalamus, and reticular formation.

These systems form the affective foundation of consciousness, generating the subjective sense of significance of events. Animals display corresponding behavioral and physiological markers — emotional expression through movement, vocalization, heart rate changes, and hormonal shifts.

Interstructural interactions between limbic–cortical networks enable the integration of emotional and cognitive processes, providing the substrate for subjective experience. For instance, activity in the cingulate gyrus and amygdala correlates with stimulus evaluation and decision-making, indicating a close link between emotion and consciousness.

6.2. Emotions and Cognitive Networks

Emotions in animals do not exist in isolation; they are tightly coupled with cognitive information processing. The integration of emotion and cognition supports:

adaptive decision-making,

risk–benefit evaluation,

prediction of the consequences of actions.

For example, studies in rats show that learning with positive reinforcement activates the SEEKING system, while aversive stimuli activate the FEAR system. This activation is accompanied by cognitive evaluation of the situation and the formation of future behavioral strategies (Balleine & O'Doherty, 2010).

Recent work highlights the role of rhythmic synchronization between limbic and cortical structures: during emotionally significant events, β- and γ-rhythm coherence increases, facilitating the integration of emotional and cognitive information.

6.3. Emotional Consciousness and Social Behavior

Emotions in animals have vital social functions. They enable:

coordination of group actions,

formation of social bonds,

prediction of conspecifics' behavior.

Examples include:

maternal care in rats and primates (**CARE**),

social play in dogs and corvids (**PLAY**),

manifestations of grief and separation anxiety (**PANIC/GRIEF**) in elephants and dolphins (Plotnik et al., 2006; Reiss & Marino, 2001).

These observations support the hypothesis that emotional awareness represents a fundamental stage in the development of subjective experience, providing the foundation for higher forms of cognitive consciousness.

6.4. Comparison with Human Emotional Consciousness

In humans, emotional consciousness is accompanied by advanced verbal reflection, empathy, and moral evaluation. In animals, these processes appear as affective self-reflection and social anticipation. The underlying neural mechanisms are largely similar: activation of limbic structures, the cingulate and prefrontal cortices, and synchronization across multiple frequency bands (Panksepp, 2011).

The primary difference lies in the level of metacognition: in animals, emotional consciousness remains mainly **primary** (Edelman, 2004), whereas in humans, it is integrated with reflective and abstract cognitive processes.

7. COMPARATIVE ANALYSIS OF HUMAN AND ANIMAL CONSCIOUSNESS

Comparative studies of consciousness make it possible to identify evolutionary continua, shared neurophysiological mechanisms, and the unique features of human awareness. The main approach involves comparing cognitive, emotional, and network components, as outlined in the previous sections.

7.1. Continuum of Consciousness Levels

From an evolutionary perspective, consciousness can be viewed as a continuum:

1. **Primary consciousness** (Edelman, 2004) — the ability to perceive the world *here and now*, integrating sensory, motor, and emotional streams. It is present in most mammals, birds, and, in simpler forms, some reptiles.
2. **Reflective (secondary) consciousness** — includes metamemory, awareness of oneself as an acting subject, and the ability to plan future actions. Found in primates, dolphins, corvids, and some elephants.
3. **Tertiary or abstract consciousness** — unique to humans: characterized by linguistic reflection, abstract reasoning, moral judgment, and cultural transmission of experience.

From the standpoint of network neurophysiology, differences between these levels correspond to the degree of global neural network integration, the coordination of interhemispheric activity, and dominant cortical rhythms (Lobasyuk, 2021).

7.2. Comparison of Cognitive Components

In animals, the cognitive functions of consciousness manifest through:

attention and orientation,

spatial thinking and planning,

tool use,

understanding of others' perspectives (a partial Theory of Mind).

In humans, these functions are complemented by:

symbolic representation of objects and actions,

linguistic reflection,

abstract reasoning and logical planning.

Modern research indicates homology of neural structures: the prefrontal cortex of humans and primates performs similar functions in integrating sensory and cognitive streams, although the complexity of connections and the density of neuronal ensembles are significantly higher in humans (Fuster, 2008).

7.3. Comparison of Emotional Components

Emotions form the foundation of consciousness in all vertebrates. In animals, they underlie:

reactive evaluation of stimuli,

adaptive behavior,

social coordination.

In humans, emotional processes are integrated with cognitive reflection, enabling:

awareness of emotions,

impulse control,

moral judgment,

behavioral planning based on internal values (Damasio, 1999).

Ukrainian and Russian studies (Lobasyuk, Sudakov, Sokolov) emphasize that emotional integration in animals occurs through network synchronization of limbic and cortical structures, forming an "affective consciousness." In humans, this network is expanded by linguistic and associative circuits, which ensure reflective awareness of one's experiences.

7.4. Network and Neurophysiological Differences

The network mechanisms of consciousness in animals and humans share several common features:

γ- and β-synchronization for integrating sensory and cognitive streams,

the reticular system and thalamocortical loops that maintain wakefulness,

interhemispheric asymmetry as an indicator of cognitive flexibility.

Human distinctions include:

higher density of associative connections,

an increased role of the anterior cingulate and prefrontal cortices,

the ability for linguistic and abstract integration,

the development of a "global workspace," where information becomes accessible to multiple cognitive modules simultaneously (Dehaene & Naccache, 2001).

Thus, the neurophysiological and network foundations of human consciousness represent a quantitative and partially qualitative elaboration of evolutionary mechanisms already identified in animals.

7.5. Evolutionary and Functional Conclusions

Comparative analysis allows the following conclusions:

1. Consciousness is the result of the evolutionary integration of sensory, motor, emotional, and cognitive systems.
2. The emotional basis of consciousness in all vertebrates is formed through limbic networks.
3. Cognitive reflection and metacognition emerge in mammals with a developed neocortex and thalamocortical loops.
4. Human consciousness represents a unique stage in the evolutionary continuum, characterized by abstract, linguistic, and reflective integration, yet relying on common network principles already observed in animals (Lobasyuk, 2025; Edelman, 2004).

Thus, humans and animals exist along a single evolutionary continuum of consciousness, differing in their level of integration, degree of reflexivity, and development of linguistic and abstract mechanisms.

8. INTEGRATIVE MODEL OF CONSCIOUSNESS

An analysis of the evolutionary, cognitive, emotional, and neurophysiological components of consciousness in animals and humans allows for the formulation of a holistic model that reflects the key principles of its organization.

8.1. Integrative Model

Consciousness can be represented as a network system composed of several levels:

1. **Sensory level** — perception of the environment and primary information processing in sensory cortical zones and the thalamus.
2. **Emotional-value level** — limbic structures (hippocampus, amygdala, cingulate cortex) forming the affective coloration of events, motivation, and basic reactions.
3. **Cognitive-reflective level** — associative zones of the neocortex and prefrontal cortex, providing planning, metacognition, Theory of Mind, and internal modeling of actions.
4. **Network integration level** — global synchronization of rhythms (α, β, γ), interhemispheric coordination, and dynamic organization of neuronal ensembles that ensure the coherence of conscious experience.

Lobasyuk (2021–2025) emphasizes that consciousness is not localized in any single structure but results from the self-organization of a network in which each node performs a cognitive-emotional function, and integration gives rise to the phenomenon of subjective experience.

8.2. Evolutionary Continuum of Consciousness

The available data confirm that animal and human consciousness form a continuous evolutionary continuum:

In lower vertebrates and some invertebrates, **primary consciousness** emerges — the integration of sensory and motor information with basic emotional reactions.

In higher mammals and birds, **reflective consciousness** develops, including metacognition, planning, and social anticipation.

In humans, **abstract, symbolic, and linguistic consciousness** arises, integrating cognitive and emotional components with a high level of reflection and cultural knowledge transmission.

8.3. Comparison of Human and Animal Consciousness

Component	Animals	Humans
Sensory integration	High but localized	High, global, and reflective
Emotional basis	Primary, affective	Integrated with cognitive reflection
Cognitive flexibility	Planning, metacognition	Planning, abstraction, language
Self-reflection	Partial, through behavior and metacognition	Full, including linguistic and symbolic forms
Network mechanisms	Interstructural rhythm synchronization	Complex global integration, γ-rhythms

As can be seen, human consciousness represents a qualitative complication of the same network and neurophysiological mechanisms that exist in animals, but it reaches the level of abstract reflection and linguistic representation.

8.4. Functional Significance of Consciousness

Consciousness performs several key functions:

1. **Adaptive function** — integration of sensory, emotional, and cognitive information for optimal behavior.
2. **Predictive function** — modeling of future events and forecasting the consequences of actions.
3. **Social function** — coordination of actions within a group, empathy, and Theory of Mind.
4. **Motivational function** — formation of internal values and behavioral priorities through emotional systems.

These functions are implemented through a dynamic neural network capable of self-organization, flexible reconfiguration, and integration of heterogeneous information.

8.5. Research Perspectives

Modern methods of network neurophysiology, cognitive ethology, and comparative psychology open new possibilities for studying consciousness in animals and humans:

topological and correlational analysis of neural networks;

experimental assessment of metacognition and planning;

integration of EEG, fMRI, and behavioral data;

study of the influence of chemical modulators (neurotransmitters, hormones) on the dynamics of conscious states.

Ukrainian and Russian studies (Lobasyuk, Sudakov, Sokolov) confirm that the network approach allows cognitive, emotional, and motor processes to be linked into a unified model, bringing us closer to understanding the phenomenology of consciousness.

Consciousness in animals and humans is a **network integration** of sensory, emotional, and cognitive processes that evolves from primary forms to reflective and abstract ones. The main distinction of the human mind lies in the **level of integration**, the capacity for linguistic and abstract reflection — yet the underlying neurophysiological principles remain common.

This **integrative model** paves the way for further understanding of the mechanisms of consciousness, its evolution, and its functional role in the behavior of animals and humans.

Table 1. Authors and Their Contribution to the Development of Theoretical Foundations of Consciousness

Section of Chapter	Source	Brief Reference in Text
1. Fundamentals of the Neurophysiology of Consciousness	Edelman & Tononi (2000)	Theory of integrative consciousness and network brain organization
	Dehaene (2014)	Global workspace theory, neurophysiological basis of consciousness
	Lobasyuk (2015)	Network approach, hemispheric asymmetry, rhythm coherence

Section of Chapter	Source	Brief Reference in Text
2. Thalamocortical and Reticular Mechanisms	Llinás (2001)	Role of thalamocortical loops in consciousness integration
	Steriade (1996)	Reticular formation and maintenance of wakefulness
	Lobasyuk & Bartsevich (2019)	Inter-structural rhythm synchronization and cognitive flow integration
3. Neural Correlates of Consciousness	Crick & Koch (1990)	Neural correlates of consciousness (NCC), neuronal markers of awareness
	Buckner, Andrews-Hanna & Schacter (2008)	Default Mode Network (DMN) and self-reflection
	Lobasyuk (2010)	Dynamics of hemispheric asymmetry as an indicator of network integration
4. Cognitive Manifestations of Consciousness	Gallup (1970)	Mirror test as an indicator of self-awareness
	Smith, Shields & Washburn (1995)	Metamemory and confidence evaluation in monkeys
	Bugnyar (2011)	Theory of Mind in ravens and behavioral prediction
	Lobasyuk & Zamkova (2023)	Interhemispheric synchronization in planning and cognitive reflection
5. Emotional and Affective Consciousness	Panksepp (1998)	Basic emotional systems in mammals
	Plotnik, de Waal & Reiss (2006)	Mirror test and emotional awareness in elephants
	Lobasyuk (2015)	Network mechanisms of cognitive and emotional integration
6. Comparative Analysis	Dehaene & Naccache (2001)	Global workspace theory, integration of cognitive processes
	Edelman (2004)	Evolution of consciousness, primary and secondary consciousness
	Lobasyuk (2019)	Network basis of cognitive and emotional consciousness, hemispheric asymmetry

9. HUMAN CONSCIOUSNESS: NEUROPHYSIOLOGICAL, COGNITIVE, AND COMPARATIVE ASPECTS

Human consciousness is a key concept in psychology, neurophysiology, and cognitive science. It integrates the subjective experience of perception, emotion, thinking, and self-awareness, ensuring adaptive interaction with the external environment and social communication (Block, 1995; Tononi, 2004).

The scientific study of consciousness lies at the intersection of philosophy, cognitive science, and neurophysiology, and is also pursued in a comparative perspective — to identify the evolutionary features of the human mind.

In philosophy, psychology, and neuroscience, several types of consciousness are distinguished depending on criteria such as level of development, content, function, and subject. The main classifications are presented below.

1. By Level of Development

1. **Sensory consciousness** — associated with perceiving the world through the senses (sensations, perceptions).
2. **Rational (logical) consciousness** — based on thinking, abstraction, and concepts.
3. **Reflective consciousness** — awareness not only of the external world but also of one's own thoughts, feelings, and actions.

2. By Subject (Carrier)

1. **Individual consciousness** — personal, subjective perception of the world.
2. **Group (collective) consciousness** — shared awareness within a small group or professional community.
3. **Social consciousness** — the totality of ideas, views, and values inherent to society as a whole.

3. By Content and Orientation

1. **Practical consciousness** — directed toward activity and transformation of the world.
2. **Theoretical consciousness** — reflects the world through concepts, theories, and scientific models.
3. **Aesthetic, moral, religious, political, legal, etc.** — forms of social consciousness differentiated by content.

4. By State

1. **Waking consciousness** — active perception and interaction with reality.
2. **Sleep (including dreaming)** — a weakened connection with the external world.
3. **Altered states of consciousness** — under the influence of hypnosis, meditation, drugs, trance, etc.

5. By Level of Self-Awareness

1. **Consciousness without self-reflection** (animals, infants).
2. **Consciousness with self-awareness** — a person perceives themselves as an "I" and is capable of self-analysis.

Philosophers distinguish between **phenomenal consciousness (qualia)** — subjective experience — and **access consciousness**, which refers to the processing of information and its integration into cognitive processes (Block, 1995; Chalmers, 1996). Cognitive science views consciousness as the result of information integration by the brain, particularly in the context of attention, working memory, and the global workspace (Baars, 1988; Dehaene & Changeux, 2011).

Neurophysiological studies have revealed that consciousness is closely related to the activity of the prefrontal, parietal, and medial cortical areas, synchronization of gamma rhythms, and functional connections within thalamo-cortical networks (Engel & Singer, 2001; Koch et al., 2016). These data make it possible to view consciousness as an integrative brain function that unites inner experience, cognitive abilities, and social interaction.

9.1. Philosophical and Theoretical Approaches

Philosophical analysis of consciousness focuses on **phenomenal experience** and **information access** (Block, 1995). Phenomenal consciousness reflects subjective experiences — color, sound, pain, emotions. Access consciousness enables cognitive functions, including planning, action, and verbal expression.

David Chalmers (1996) distinguishes between the **"hard problem"** of consciousness — the question of how subjective experience arises from physical brain activity — and the **"easy problems"**, which concern the study of the neurophysiological correlates of consciousness.

Ukrainian researchers (Kovalchuk T.M. et al., 2019) emphasize the role of cognitive integration, linking consciousness with functional brain networks, particularly with cortico-thalamic loops. Lobasyuk B.A. (2010) studies the systemic mechanisms of brain electrogenesis and their relationship to cognitive and emotional states, which makes it possible to integrate local cortical rhythms with global conscious experience.

9.2. Cognitive Approach

Cognitive models view consciousness as a product of the **global workspace** (Baars, 1988; Dehaene & Changeux, 2011). Information becomes conscious when it is integrated and available for verbal representation, action planning, and coordination of cognitive processes.

Working memory ensures the retention and manipulation of information, allowing for reflective states and self-awareness. Neurophysiologically, this is manifested in the activation of the **dorsolateral prefrontal cortex** and **parietal areas** (Miller & Cohen, 2001).

Cognitive scientists emphasize the importance of integrative work between sensory systems and associative cortical areas in forming conscious experience.

9.3. Neurophysiological Mechanisms

Consciousness is associated with the activation of **top-down frontal networks**, the **medial prefrontal cortex**, the **posterior cingulate gyrus**, and **thalamo-cortical loops** (Tononi, 2004; Koch et al., 2016). **EEG** studies show that conscious perception is accompanied by synchronization of **gamma rhythms** (Engel & Singer, 2001).

The **Integrated Information Theory (IIT)** (Tononi, 2004) states that consciousness arises from a high degree of informational connectivity in the brain, when numerous neural networks integrate local signals into a global cognitive field.

Lobasyuk B.A. (2015) demonstrated that **interhemispheric asymmetries** and **rhythmic coordination of cortical regions** determine the level of cognitive integration and subjective experience.

9.4. Evolutionary and Comparative Aspects

Human consciousness is distinguished by a high degree of **self-reflection** and **metacognition**, which manifests in the ability for **abstract thinking**, **language**, and understanding **others' mental states** (Premack & Woodruff, 1978).

Comparative studies show that **primates** possess basic self-awareness (for example, the **mirror test**), while **dolphins** and certain **bird species** exhibit elements of **planning** and **social cognition**. However, the uniqueness of **human consciousness** lies in the development of **language**, **culture**, and **complex social organization**.

Ukrainian authors, including **Lobasyuk** and **Bodelan**, emphasize the importance of **intercortical networks** and **neural rhythms** in forming complex cognitive functions that are characteristic only of *Homo sapiens*.

9.5. Self-Awareness and the "Self" Neural Networks

Self-awareness is formed through the activity of the **medial prefrontal cortex**, **posterior cingulate gyrus**, and **parahippocampal region**. These structures integrate internal experience with external information, enabling the formation of a **subjective sense of self** (Northoff et al., 2006).

Neurophysiological studies show that activation of these networks is accompanied by increased synchronization of **gamma** and **theta rhythms**, reflecting a high degree of **information integration** necessary for **self-reflection** and **decision-making**.

9.6. Pathologies of Consciousness

Pathologies of consciousness — such as comas, minimally conscious states, dementia, and neurodegenerative diseases — provide a unique opportunity to study the correlates of consciousness. Research shows that the loss of consciousness is associated with disruption of interhemispheric coordination and degradation of fronto-parietal networks (Laureys et al., 2004).

Lobasyuk and colleagues (2022) note that disturbances in rhythmic cortical coordination in brain pathologies lead to fragmentation of cognitive integration, which is reflected at the level of subjective experience.

Human consciousness is a multidisciplinary phenomenon that unites subjective experience, cognitive processes, and neurophysiological mechanisms. To date, there is no unified theory that fully explains all aspects of consciousness; however, the synthesis of philosophical, cognitive, and neurophysiological data allows for the gradual formation of an integrative understanding of this phenomenon.

Pathology of consciousness refers to a set of disorders in which the normal characteristics of consciousness are altered: level of wakefulness, clarity, content, self-awareness, orientation, and the ability to perceive reality. These disturbances may arise in psychiatric, neurological, toxic, metabolic, and other conditions.

Main Characteristics of Normal Consciousness

Clarity: The presence of clear and consistent perception of the surrounding world and correct orientation within it, i.e., allo-orientation, autopsychic orientation, and the presence of self-awareness with preservation of memory for past and present events, as well as the ability to take responsibility for and control one's actions.

Breadth: A certain number of associations or experiences that are present in consciousness at a given time, i.e., the extent to which consciousness encompasses the surrounding situation and one's own experiences.

Content: The associations that arise under the influence of various stimuli and are present in consciousness — that is, the content of thoughts and experiences.

Continuity: The unity of past, present, and future experiences.

Symptoms of Disturbance of Consciousness

(*K. Jaspers, 1948*)

Complete inability to perceive the external world, or perception that is fragmentary and unclear.

Disordered thinking (disjointed, chaotic), with impaired analysis and synthesis.

Complete or partial disorientation in place, time, and self.

Amnestic disturbances covering the period of impaired consciousness.

Paroxysmal onset of psychopathological symptoms, which disappear as suddenly as they appear, corresponding to changes in the etiological factor (e.g., epileptic seizure).

Disorders of Consciousness

Quantitative Disorders (impairments or loss of consciousness):

Stupor (Clouding of consciousness)

Obnubilatio

Somnolenc

Sopor

Coma

Absence

Syncope (fainting, loss of consciousness)

Qualitative Disorders (disturbances of consciousness content):

Delirium

Amentia

Oneiroid state

Twilight state — includes ambulatory automatism, fugues, trances, somnambulism (sleepwalking).

Special states of consciousness — a type of twilight state: a) Pathological affect;

b) Pathological intoxication;

c) Pathological hypnagogic (presleep) state;

d) "Short-circuit" reaction;

e) Syndromes of "déjà vu" and "jamais vu," "déjà entendu" and "jamais entendu."

Quantitative Disorders

Obnubilation (*from Latin nubes — cloud*) — the mildest degree of clouding. The patient transitions from a clear state of consciousness to incomplete understanding of what is happening. Responses are slow; comprehension of the situation is reduced; behavior is sluggish.

Somnolence — increased threshold for perception of external stimuli. The patient does not respond to a quiet voice, reacts slowly to loud speech, performs simple tasks slowly, and cannot comprehend complex ones. Facial expression is blank, reactions to pain are reduced.

Sopor (*stupor, deep sleep*) — may occur independently or follow obnubilation. The patient appears to be in deep sleep, with no meaningful contact possible. All forms of orientation are lost. Strong stimuli (pain, sound) evoke elementary, uncomprehending reactions. Unconditioned reflexes are preserved (pain, pupillary, corneal, swallowing).

Coma (*profound sleep, no memory*) — the deepest degree of unconsciousness. Complete absence of reaction to external stimuli and loss of unconditioned reflexes. Disturbances of respiration, cardiac activity, and other vital functions occur. Psychomotor agitation or epileptiform seizures may be present. Complete amnesia follows.

Types of coma: hyperglycemic, renal, hepatic, thyrotoxic, alcoholic, post-traumatic, etc.

Causes of loss of consciousness: severe intoxication, traumatic brain injury, organic CNS lesions, severe somatic illness, epileptic seizures.

Absence (*from French "absence" — lapse*) — brief (2–5 seconds) loss of consciousness as a manifestation of epilepsy.

Syncope (fainting) — loss of consciousness due to decreased cerebral blood flow (e.g., from blood loss, emotional shock, or confined space).

Qualitative Disorders (Confusional States)

Delirium (*from Latin delirare — to be deranged*)

Allo-orientation is impaired, but auto-orientation is preserved. Characterized by vivid (usually visual) hallucinations and delusions (often of persecution). Hallucinations are typically frightening, isolated or panoramic, accompanied by affect of fear. The patient behaves according to the hallucinations (defending, attacking), and may be dangerous to self or others.

The condition worsens in the evening and at night; "lucid intervals" may occur during the day.

Marked autonomic disturbances (flushing, pallor, tachycardia) are observed.

In alcoholism, hallucinations are often black-and-white, with microzoohallucinations (devils, rats, insects).

In epilepsy (epileptic delirium), hallucinations are vivid, colorful (blood, flames), and often religious in content. The episode ends with amnesia, though the brightest visions are sometimes recalled. Duration: 2–5–7 days.

Atypical forms of alcoholic delirium may include:

Muttering delirium (mussitating type)

Professional delirium

Amentia

(from Latin — "nonsense")

Amentia is an acute confusional state characterized by disruption of the synthetic activity of thought with partial preservation of analytic functions. As a result, speech becomes incoherent, and comprehension of the environment is absent — that is, **primary incoherence of thinking (incoherence)** is observed.

Fragmentary hallucinations and delusional ideas are typical, especially in the evening and at night.

All forms of orientation are disturbed. The patient may exhibit restlessness or agitation, usually confined to the bed.

It occurs in severe somatic and infectious diseases, sepsis, and postpartum psychoses.

Oneiroid State

(from Latin — "dream")

Characterized by dream-like, fantastic hallucinations — specifically **pseudohallucinations**, in which the events occur as if in a mental space rather than in external reality.

Illusory and hallucinatory phenomena are extremely vivid and unusual. The delusions are of a **fantastic content** — for example, "travels through Rome," or "flights into space."

Orientation is completely disrupted or **dual** (the patient simultaneously experiences both real and fantastic worlds).

The patient takes **an active part** in these fantastic events. Subjective perception of time is distorted — it may seem to pass extremely quickly (thousands of years, multiple civilizations) or very slowly.

Observed in: **schizophrenia (oneiroid catatonia), epilepsy, organic brain lesions.**

Twilight State of Consciousness

A **pathologically narrowed state of consciousness** that arises suddenly.

Characterized by vivid hallucinations, delusional ideas, psychomotor agitation, and aggression corresponding to the delusional plot.

Complete amnesia and total disorientation follow.

Occurs in: **epilepsy, organic brain damage, hysterical psychoses.**

Subtype — Ambulatory Automatism

A form of twilight consciousness **without hallucinations or delusions**; outward behavior appears organized.

Types of Ambulatory Automatism:

Trance: The patient may travel for long periods, appearing absent-minded. When found in a new place, they cannot recall how they got there. Complete amnesia for the episode.

Fugue *(from Latin fuga — "flight")*: An uncontrollable impulse to run, occurring against the background of a twilight state. Lasts minutes and ends abruptly. Complete amnesia.

Occurs in: **epilepsy, organic brain lesions.**

Somnambulism (Sleepwalking) *(from Latin "sleep-walking")*: A twilight state arising during sleep. The child (sometimes adult) rises during sleep, walks around, may go outside, even overcome dangerous obstacles (e.g., walking along a ledge) without fear. Complete amnesia. Should not be awakened (may cause panic).

Occurs in: **neuroses, epilepsy, organic brain lesions.**

Special States of Consciousness

(A subtype of twilight state)

Pathological Affect:

A short-term, intense emotional reaction to a minor stimulus, accompanied by clouding of consciousness, aggression, CNS exhaustion, followed by deep sleep and complete amnesia.

Occurs in: **organic CNS lesions, excitable (explosive) personality disorders (psychopathy).**

Pathological Intoxication:

After ingestion of a small dose of alcohol — with no signs of ordinary intoxication — an acute clouding of consciousness occurs, accompanied by aggression and dangerous actions. Ends with sleep and complete amnesia. Occurs in: **organic brain lesions, psychopathy, asthenic states.**

Pathological Hypnagogic (Presleep) State:

Occurs in guards or sentries while on duty. The person appears not fully awake: the sense of self ("I") awakens first, but allo-orientation (awareness of surroundings) is delayed.

The individual may, for example, use a weapon in this state.

"Short-Circuit" Reaction:

Against a background of long-standing emotional tension or trauma, a minor stimulus may provoke a sudden, violent, and inadequate reaction with aggression and dangerous actions.

All such individuals are considered **not responsible (insane)** for their actions.

"Already Seen" and "Never Seen" States:

("Déjà vu," "Jamais vu," "Déjà entendu," "Jamais entendu") — may occur in **neuroses and epilepsy.**

Major Psychopathological Syndromes

Symptom → Syndrome: simple → complex

As the severity of mental disturbance increases, syndromes may be arranged as follows:

1. **Asthenic Syndrome**
2. **Affective Syndromes:**

Depressive

Manic

3. **Neurotic Syndromes:**

Hysterical

Obsessive-compulsive

Senesto-hypochondriacal

Depersonalization

Dysmorphophobic

4. **Paranoid Syndrome**
5. **Hallucinosis**
6. **Hallucinatory-Paranoid Syndrome**, including **Kandinsky–Clérambault Syndrome:**

Ideational (associative) variant

Senestopathic variant

Motor (kinesthetic) variant

7. **Paraphrenic Syndrome**
8. **Catatonic Syndrome**
9. **Disorders of Consciousness:**

Quantitative (loss or suppression)

Qualitative (clouding)

10. **Convulsive Syndromes**
11. **Psychoorganic (Amnestic) Syndrome**

9.7. Theories of Consciousness

9.7.1. Global Workspace Theory (GWT)

Main idea. Consciousness arises when information is "broadcast" into a **global workspace**—that is, when separate brain modules gain access to a central "stage" of processing, like a "theater of the mind." In this metaphor, multiple subsystems compete, and whatever "comes on stage" becomes conscious content.

Why it matters. The theory is well-articulated and supported by **neuroscientific evidence** concerning **broad neural networks**, **information access**, and **cognitive integration**. It provides a convenient **functional explanation** of consciousness in terms of **accessibility**, **reportability**, and **information processing**.

Criticism / limitations. The theory explains **information accessibility** better than **qualitative experience**—that is, why a given state **feels** a certain way subjectively.

Key references:

The Neuroscience of Consciousness (Stanford Encyclopedia of Philosophy) — section on GWT.

Human Consciousness: Where Is It From and What Is It For — review article.

9.7.2. Integrated Information Theory (IIT)

Main idea.

Consciousness is a measure of how much a system integrates information (represented by "Φ" — *phi*). The greater the integration and the harder it is to divide the system into independent parts, the higher its level of consciousness.

Why it matters.

IIT attempts to connect a purely subjective phenomenon (the feeling of self or experience) with a quantitative measure. It also extends beyond humans — for example, it allows discussion of the possible states of consciousness in animals or machines.

Criticism / limitations.

It is very difficult to empirically measure "Φ" in real systems. Moreover, the theory can lead to **panpsychist** conclusions — that even simple systems may possess some minimal degree of consciousness — which is controversial.

Key references:

Stanford Encyclopedia of Philosophy — section on IIT.

"Most Widely Accepted and Promising Theories of Consciousness" — overview article.

Attention Schema Theory (AST)

Main idea.

Developed by neuroscientist **Michael Graziano**, this theory proposes that consciousness is a kind of *schema* (or model) of attention that the brain constructs to monitor and control its own attentional processes. The subjective feeling of "I am aware" results from the operation of this internal model.

Why it matters.

AST connects attention — a well-studied concept in psychology and neuroscience — with subjective awareness. It also explains *why* we feel that we are aware: because the brain has built a model of that very process.

Criticism / limitations.

The theory is still relatively new and not as thoroughly tested as GWT or IIT. Some argue that it explains only part of consciousness (for instance, attentional aspects) but not its full phenomenology.

Main Theories of Consciousness

Table 2. Overview of several leading theories

Theory / Hypothesis	Brief Description
Global Workspace Theory (GWT)	Consciousness arises when information becomes "globally available" to multiple subsystems of the brain through a common "workspace." Once information enters this global workspace, it becomes conscious.
Integrated Information Theory (IIT)	Consciousness is measured by the degree of integration and information within a system. The higher the integration and the more information that cannot be reduced to the system's parts, the stronger the consciousness.
Higher-Order Thought / Representation (HOT)	Consciousness is not only the presence of sensory information but also the system's representation *of being aware* of that information — "we know that we know."
Recurrent / Reentrant Processing Theory	Consciousness requires feedback (recurrent connections) within sensory streams and between processing levels, not just a one-way feedforward flow from stimuli to perception.
Predictive Processing / Predictive Coding Theory	Consciousness is related to how the brain predicts sensory inputs and updates its internal model of the world. Prediction errors can become conscious signals.
Physical / Quantum Proposals	Less mainstream and more speculative theories that attempt to link consciousness to fundamental physics or quantum effects.

Why IIT Appears Particularly Promising

It offers a **quantitative metric** — the degree of consciousness as "integrated information" (Φ).

It can be applied not only to humans but also to **other systems** (AI, possibly animals), making it a universal framework.

It addresses a **fundamental question**: what distinguishes a conscious state from a merely complex computational system — not just reaction, but an indivisible whole of information.

At the same time, the **Global Workspace Theory** also seems highly practical and experimentally supported: many findings show activation of **frontal and temporal networks** when a person becomes aware of something, consistent with GWT predictions.

Table 3. Comparative Analysis of Major Theories of Human Consciousness

№	Hypothesis / Theory	Core Idea	Main Representatives	Strengths	Weaknesses
1	**Global Neuronal Workspace Theory (GNWT)**	Consciousness arises when information becomes globally accessible to multiple specialized brain subsystems through long-range neural networks (mainly frontal and parietal areas).	B. Baars (1988), S. Dehaene, J.-P. Changeux (2011–2021)	Supported by neurophysiological data (fMRI, EEG, ERP); explains *access consciousness*; fits cognitive and attentional frameworks.	Does not solve the "hard problem" (subjectivity of experience); focuses mainly on cognitive, not phenomenological, aspects.
2	**Integrated Information Theory (IIT)**	Consciousness is a measure of integrated information in a system (Φ); the higher the integration, the richer the phenomenal experience.	G. Tononi (2004–2024), C. Koch	Offers a formal quantitative index (Φ); bridges neuroscience and philosophy; accounts for phenomenal experience.	Hard to test experimentally; implies panpsychist conclusions (any complex system might have some consciousness).
3	**Higher-Order Thought Theory (HOT)**	Consciousness arises when a system becomes aware of its own mental states; meta-representations generate the subjective "self."	D. Rosenthal, P. Carruthers	Explains reflexivity and metacognition; fits data on prefrontal activation.	Does not explain primary phenomenal experience; mainly philosophical with limited neural grounding.
4	**Predictive Processing / Bayesian Brain Theory**	The brain is a prediction machine; consciousness arises from balancing expectations and sensory prediction errors.	K. Friston, A. Clark (2018–2024)	Integrates consciousness, attention, and perception into a unified computational framework; explains illusions and perceptual anomalies.	Mathematically complex; does not fully capture subjective qualities.

№	Hypothesis / Theory	Core Idea	Main Representatives	Strengths	Weaknesses
5	**Orchestrated Objective Reduction (Orch-OR) — Quantum Hypothesis**	Consciousness results from quantum processes in neuronal microtubules.	R. Penrose, S. Hameroff	Original attempt to unite quantum physics and biology; stimulates search for a physical substrate of subjectivity.	Lacks empirical support; quantum effects in neurons remain doubtful.

The most empirically supported and heuristically productive theory in contemporary science is the **Global Neuronal Workspace Theory (GNWT)**. It integrates findings from neurophysiology, cognitive psychology, and information theory, while allowing for potential synthesis with other models (for example, **IIT** for phenomenology and **predictive theory** for computational description).

10. THE UNCONSCIOUS IN SIGMUND FREUD'S THEORY

10.1. Historical and Scientific Background

Consciousness is not the primary attribute of the psyche—it represents its highest form. Alongside conscious, or consciously experienced, mental processes, there exists a class of **unconscious (non-conscious) mental phenomena** that are highly significant for the execution of functions and behavior (Chkharishvili Sh.N., 1978).

As Bassin F.V. writes, *"The idea of the unconscious, as in a peculiar focal point, brings together very different lines of development in philosophical and scientific thought. As a result of this convergence, there arises a characteristic 'interdisciplinarity' of the concept of the unconscious—its connection to a wide range of specialized fields of knowledge, from the theory of biological regulation, neuro- and electrophysiology to the psychology of creativity, art theory, questions of social psychology, and even pedagogy."* (Bassin F.V.)

The **"unconscious"**, as a non-conscious mental process, participates in organizing purposeful behavior without becoming the direct content of the subject's consciousness (Waldman A.V., 1983).

In 19th-century psychology, two distinct approaches to understanding the unconscious had already emerged. One, the **"negative"** approach (Bassin F.V., 1968), viewed the unconscious as a diminished form of conscious clarity. The second, the **"positive"** approach, as defined by F.V. Bassin, regarded the unconscious as a *qualitatively distinct latent activity of the brain*, capable, under certain conditions, of exerting a profound influence on behavior and complex forms of adaptation (Bassin F.V., 1968).

A major contribution not only to the sciences that study mental activity but also to human culture as a whole was the **doctrine of psychoanalysis**, created by **Sigmund Freud**.

Fig. 6. Sigmund Freud *(also acceptable: Freud; German: Sigmund Freud, IPA [ˈziːkmʊnt ˈfʁɔʏt]; full name Sigismund Schlomo Freud; May 6, 1856, Freiberg, Austrian Empire — September 23, 1939, London) — Austrian psychologist, psychiatrist, and neurologist (Wikipedia).*

Freud discovered that beneath the veil of consciousness lies a deep, "boiling" layer of unconscious, unacknowledged yet powerful drives, impulses, and desires (Yaroshevsky M.G., 1990).

In his *Lectures on Psychoanalysis*, Freud stated:

"Through the study of hypnotic phenomena we have become accustomed to an idea that at first seemed utterly strange to us—namely, that within one and the same individual, several mental groupings may coexist, which can exist in a person quite independently of one another, may 'know' nothing of each other, and may alternately take possession of consciousness. Cases of this kind, known as *double conscience* (split consciousness), sometimes occur spontaneously. If, in such a splitting of the personality, consciousness remains constantly attached to only one of the two states, then this latter is called the *conscious* mental state, and the one separated from it—the *unconscious*."

(*Freud, 1990*).

Freud's metaphorical comparison has long since become famous: the *Id* (the unconscious) is the **horse**, while the *Ego* (the conscious mind) is the **rider** who must rein in a creature far stronger than himself.

"If the rider does not wish to part with the horse, he has no choice but to guide it where it wants to go. Our *Ego* carries out the will of the *Id* as if it were its own," wrote the founder of psychoanalysis in one of his works.

Modern neuroscientists have reached similar conclusions. In most cases, it is the **unconscious** that determines human actions, while our **consciousness** merely attributes these unconscious intentions to itself, reinterpreting them after the fact so that we do not recoil in confusion before the inexplicable motives of our behavior.

"In our heads, an interpretive machine is constantly at work—its goal is to find an explanation for everything," says Michael Gazzaniga.

Consciousness, as Vygotsky wrote (Vygotsky L.S., 1982), is characterized by interruptions and often lacks visible connections between its separate elements. The concept of the unconscious fills the gaps between conscious phenomena and allows the study of all human mental functions—even their highest forms—from a deterministic perspective. The unconscious is as much a **psychological reality** as the conscious (Alexandrov Yu.I., 1995).

With the advent of computer technologies, it has become possible to quickly analyze large volumes of information. This, in turn, has enabled the development of fundamentally new approaches to studying mental processes and their disorders (Shevrin H., Williams W.J., Marshall R.E., 1987).

The concept of the **unconscious** existed in 19th-century philosophy and psychology long before Freud—it had been discussed by Leibniz, Schopenhauer, Nietzsche, and within Romantic natural philosophy. However, it was Freud who gave the term a **scientific and psychological meaning**, linking it to the dynamics of mental processes and the mechanisms of psychopathology (*Freud, 1900*).

Freud believed that the unconscious is the **realm of repressed desires and ideas** that continue to influence human behavior despite the absence of awareness. He based this conclusion on clinical observations of patients suffering from hysteria, phobias, and obsessive states, revealing the operation of hidden conflicts between conscious and unconscious forces of the psyche (*Freud, 1915*).

10.2. The Structure of the Psyche and the Role of the Unconscious

Within the framework of Freud's **structural model of personality**, he distinguished three levels of mental organization:

- **Id (Es)** — the primary, instinctive level; the source of drives and libidinal energy. The Id is entirely unconscious and governed by the **pleasure principle**.
- **Ego (Ich)** — the rational instance, operating according to the **reality principle**; it develops from the Id and serves to adapt the individual to the external world.

- **Superego (Über-Ich)** — the internalized system of moral norms and prohibitions, assimilated from society.

In this triad, the **unconscious** represents the fundamental energetic basis of personality, from which both **psychic conflicts** and **creative impulses** arise [Freud, 1923].

10.3. Mechanisms of Repression and Dreaming

Freud regarded **repression** as the central mechanism of the unconscious — a process in which thoughts and desires unacceptable to consciousness are expelled into the unconscious but remain active, manifesting themselves in **symptoms, dreams, slips of the tongue, and mistaken actions**.

A special place in his theory is occupied by the **analysis of dreams**, which he called the *"royal road to the unconscious"* [Freud, 1900]. According to Freud, a dream is a **compromise** between the censoring consciousness and repressed desires, realized i*n symbolic form. In *The Interpretation of Dreams* (1900), he described in detail the mechanisms of **displacement** and **condensation**, through which the unconscious disguises its true impulses.

10.4. The Unconscious and Neuroses

Freud maintained that **neurotic symptoms** are substitute formations of unconscious conflicts. **Psychoanalytic therapy** aims to bring these conflicts into awareness, symbolically "replay" them, and integrate them into the structure of consciousness.

Thus, the goal of psychoanalysis is **to transform the unconscious into the conscious** — *Wo Es war, soll Ich werden* ("Where the Id was, the Ego shall be") [Freud, 1933].

10.5. Cultural and Philosophical Aspects

Freud extended the idea of the unconscious to **socio-cultural processes**, viewing **religion, art, and morality** as forms of **sublimation** of instinctual drives. In *Totem and Taboo* (1913) and *Civilization and Its Discontents* (1930), he analyzed civilization as the outcome of repressing unconscious drives and redirecting their energy into socially acceptable forms.

Modern **cognitive psychology** and **neuroscience** partially confirm the existence of unconscious behavioral regulators, although they interpret them in terms of **subconscious automatisms** rather than repressed desires (Kihlstrom, 1987; Damasio, 1999).

10.6. Criticism and Contemporary Significance

Freud's concept of the unconscious has been criticized by **K. Popper** (for its unfalsifiability) and **B.F. Skinner** (for neglecting behavioral laws). Nevertheless, it exerted a profound influence on the **humanities of the 20th century** — including philosophy, art theory, cultural studies, literary criticism, and cognitive science.

Today, Freud's ideas are regarded as a **metaphorical model of deep psychic dynamics**, relevant to the study of **symbolism, motivation, and emotional memory** [Green, 2003].

10.7. Neurophysiological Correlates of the Unconscious

Modern **neuropsychology** and **cognitive neuroscience** have broadened the understanding of the Freudian unconscious, viewing it not as an exclusively psychoanalytic category but as a **dynamic neural network system** operating outside the boundaries of conscious control.

10.7.1. The Unconscious and Brain Networks

Recent research has shown that unconscious processes are linked to the activity of specific **functional brain networks**, particularly:

The **Default Mode Network (DMN)** — including the medial prefrontal cortex, posterior cingulate cortex, hippocampus, and parietal regions — responsible for *internal representations, autobiographical memory, and spontaneous thought [Raichle et al., 2001].

The **Limbic system**, including the amygdala, hippocampus, and hypothalamus, where emotional impulses and motivational programs are formed prior to conscious awareness.

The **Basal ganglia** and **cerebellum**, which participate in unconscious motor and cognitive automatisms.

These systems sustain a **continuous background flow of preconscious activity** that structures consciousness and behavior, shaping decision-making and emotional responses [Damasio, 2010; Dehaene, 2014].

10.7.2. The Network Concept of the Unconscious in B.A. Lobasyuk's Model

Within **B.A. Lobasyuk's network neurophysiological framework**, the unconscious is viewed as an **integrative subsystem of the brain** that generates latent states of functional networks — states not manifest at the moment, yet influencing the current condition of the consciousness system [Lobasyuk, 2021].

According to Lobasyuk's **network model of consciousness**, mental states are **dynamic configurations of neuronal ensembles**, linked both topologically and semantically. Consciousness represents the **activated part** of this network, while the unconscious comprises the **"dimmed" nodes and connections** that store information about prior experience and motivational tendencies [Lobasyuk, 2024].

This approach aligns with **Stanislas Dehaene's Global Neuronal Workspace Theory**, in which unconscious processing corresponds to **local neural activity** that does not reach the level of **network synchronization** required for conscious awareness [Dehaene, 2014].

10.7.3. The Unconscious as the Basis of Cognitive Prediction

Contemporary neural models of consciousness (Friston, 2010; Seth, 2021) conceptualize the unconscious as a **predictive level of information processing**, continuously forecasting sensory input and regulating bodily states. These processes occur mostly outside awareness, yet they ensure the **stability of perception** and the **subjective sense of self**.

In this sense, the unconscious is the **physiological infrastructure of consciousness**, maintaining the continuity of cognitive experience. It is not opposed to consciousness, as in Freud's model, but rather **precedes and supports it** at a systemic level.

Thus, Freud's ideas of hidden unconscious activity have received **neurophysiological confirmation** within modern **network models of the brain**.

The unconscious is no longer seen as a repressed realm of the psyche, but as a **functionally active layer of neural interactions** that form preconscious structures upon which conscious activity is built.

Lobasyuk's **network theory** emphasizes that **consciousness and the unconscious** are two **interconnected modes** of operation of a single neural network, differing in their degree of synchronization, activation level, and topological connectivity [Lobasyuk, 2021; Lobasyuk, 2024].

10.7.4. Freud: The Unconscious as Conflict and Repression

In *The Interpretation of Dreams* (1900), Freud wrote:

"The unconscious is the true psychical reality; in its depths lie the genuine motives of human behavior."

According to Freud, the unconscious is the **result of repressing unacceptable impulses** from consciousness under the censorship of the Ego and Superego. It manifests through **symptoms, slips, dreams, and symbolic actions**, which contain encrypted traces of repressed experience.

This model presupposes a **duality**: **conscious ↔ unconscious**, a struggle between the **pleasure principle** and the **reality principle**.

The task of psychoanalysis is to **restore the repressed to consciousness** and reestablish the subject's **inner equilibrium**.

10.8. Freudian and Network Models of the Unconscious: A Comparative Analysis

10.8.1. Methodological Framework for Comparison

The **psychoanalytic concept of the unconscious**, proposed by **Sigmund Freud**, and the **modern network-based neurophysiological model** developed by **B.A. Lobasyuk** represent two distinct — yet mutually complementary — approaches to understanding the deep mechanisms of the psyche.

Freud analyzed the unconscious **phenomenologically and clinically**, as a system of **repressed representations, conflicts, and drives**. Lobasyuk, in contrast, examined it **systemically and neurodynamically**, as a **level of**

the brain's topological organization where hidden processes of cognitive structure formation and semantic connection-building occur.

For Freud, the unconscious is a **psychic force opposing consciousness**; in the **network model**, it is a **structural layer of neural organization** from which consciousness emerges as the "higher level of integration" [Lobasyuk, 2021].

10.8.2. Comparison of the Main Features of the Models

Parameter	Freudian Model	Lobasyuk's Network Model
Ontological status	Psychic reality generated by repression	Neurophysiological subsystem of the brain
Dynamics	Conflict and return of the repressed	Oscillatory activity and network synchronization
Mechanism of manifestation	Symbolization (dreams, slips, symptoms)	Activation of functional network nodes
Goal of mental regulation	Resolution of internal conflict	Maintenance of systemic balance and adaptation
Method of study	Psychoanalysis, interpretation	Electrophysiological and network modeling
Relation to consciousness	Opposed to consciousness	Serves as its basis and background

10.8.3. Conceptual Synthesis

If, in Freud's theory, the unconscious is the **dynamic shadow of mental experience**, then in the network conception it is the **architecture of possible brain states**.

The former explains **why** a person acts against themselves; the latter explains **how** these hidden processes unfold in neural dynamics.

The synthesis of these perspectives opens the way toward an **interdisciplinary model of consciousness**, in which the **psychoanalytic "depth"** is integrated with the **neurophysiological "breadth"** of network interactions.

As Freud presciently remarked, *"We are not masters in our own house"* (*Das Ich ist nicht Herr im eigenen Hause*, 1917).

Freud's theory paved the way for understanding **the psychodynamics of personality**; Lobasyuk's approach advances **the neurophysiological modeling of mental wholeness**.

In both cases, the **unconscious** functions as the **foundation of mental life**, though in different forms:

in Freud's view — as a **hidden source of motivation**,

in Lobasyuk's view — as a **latent architecture of semantic connections**.

Their synthesis gives rise to a **new paradigm of cognitive science** — the **network cognitivism of the unconscious**, integrating **psychoanalysis, neurophysiology, and systems thinking**.

11. The Unconscious as the Systemic Basis of the Psyche

11.1. From Psychoanalysis to the Neural Network Paradigm

The evolution of the concept of the unconscious demonstrates a shift from the **introspective-clinical understanding** of psychic depth (S. Freud, C.G. Jung, A. Adler) to a **neurosystemic conception** of the brain as a **self-organizing network**, in which the unconscious is not a metaphor but a **specific level of informational and energetic organization**.

Freud created the first **multilevel model of the psyche**, in which the unconscious served as the **dynamic foundation of personality**, regulating behavior and affect. This model became an **epistemological prototype** for later systemic theories.

Modern **neurosciences**, expanding upon Freud's ideas, have reinterpreted the unconscious in terms of **neural dynamics, network synchronization, and predictive mechanisms of the brain** [Friston, 2010; Dehaene, 2014; Lobasyuk, 2021].

11.2. The Unconscious as a Systemic Function

From the standpoint of **systems theory** (Anokhin, 1975; Bernstein, 1947), the unconscious can be viewed as the **functional core of mental regulation**, ensuring the automatism and stability of behavior.

This subsystem integrates **sensory, motivational, and cognitive processes** into a unified adaptive field, operating according to the **principle of anticipatory reflection** (P.K. Anokhin).

In **B.A. Lobasyuk's model (2021)**, the unconscious appears as the **background topology of brain networks**, maintaining the system's readiness for conscious activation. These "latent networks" correspond to **basic functional ensembles** identified through **EEG, fMRI**, and **neural modeling** methods.

"Consciousness is a flash of synchronization in a sea of latent interactions."
— *Lobasyuk, 2024*

11.3. Integration of Cognitive and Psychoanalytic Approaches

Freud's idea of the **"dynamic unconscious"** has received a modern interpretation within the framework of **cognitive psychology** (Kihlstrom, 1987; Bargh

& Morsella, 2008), where it refers to **unconscious mechanisms of decision-making, attentional automatisms, implicit memory**, and **emotional regulation**.

Thus, the concept of the unconscious ceases to be an exclusively psychoanalytic construct and becomes a **universal category of cognitive science** — one that describes **distributed, implicit, and self-sustaining processes of the psyche**.

Modern **cognitology** (Lobasyuk, 2022) considers consciousness and the unconscious as **hierarchically interconnected levels** of a **neural-semantic system**, in which each level encodes information with a different degree of **integration and accessibility**.

11.4. The Unconscious and Self-Consciousness

Of particular significance is the relationship between the **unconscious** and the **formation of self-awareness**.

Freud viewed the unconscious as the **source of the irrational**, but also as the **raw material** from which the Ego develops through the process of making the unconscious conscious.

Modern neurophysiology refines this view: **self-awareness arises from the backward projection of network activity** onto the subject's own representations — that is, through the **recognition of one's own unconscious information-processing acts** (Lau & Rosenthal, 2011).

Consequently, the unconscious is **not the enemy of the Ego**, but its **architect**, providing the **structural integrity** of the mental system.

11.5. The Evolutionary-Cognitive Aspect

From an **evolutionary** perspective, the unconscious can be regarded as a **primary mechanism of mental self-regulation**, which emerged long before the appearance of reflective consciousness.

In animals, as shown by **neuroethological studies** (Panksepp, 1998; Lobasyuk, 2021), unconscious reactions ensure **adaptive behavior** and **emotional stabilization**.

In humans, these ancient mechanisms have not disappeared but have become the **foundation of cognitive and symbolic activity**.

Thus, the **unconscious functions as the evolutionary substrate of the mind** — the **energetic, motivational, and semantic foundation** of all mental activity.

A comparison of the classical and modern models allows us to conclude that:

1. **Freud** discovered the **dynamic structure of the unconscious**, showing its role in the formation of personality and symptoms.
2. **Neurophysiology** identified its **objective correlates** in the form of network and rhythmic brain processes.
3. **Cognitology** gave the concept **systemic meaning**, viewing the unconscious as a **distributed informational system of adaptive behavior**.
4. **Lobasyuk's network concept** integrated these levels, demonstrating that the unconscious is a **functionally active network of latent brain states**, ensuring the **integrity of consciousness, memory, and personality**.

In this sense, the unconscious is **not the shadow of the psyche**, but its **structural core**, from which **consciousness grows as a form of higher integration**.

12. NEO-FREUDIANISM

Neo-Freudianism is a movement in psychology and psychoanalysis that emerged in the first half of the 20th century as both a **development and partial critique** of Sigmund Freud's ideas.

The Neo-Freudians accepted the main principles of Freudian theory (the unconscious, the role of childhood, defense mechanisms, etc.) but **expanded and reinterpreted** them, emphasizing **social and cultural factors** rather than biological instincts in shaping personality.

12.1. Main Differences between Neo-Freudianism and Classical Freudianism

Key representatives of Neo-Freudianism:

1. **Karen Horney** — emphasized the role of **anxiety and insecurity** arising from interpersonal relationships rather than repressed libido.
2. **Erich Fromm** — viewed humans as **social beings**, driven by the need for **love, freedom, and self-realization**.
3. **Harry Stack Sullivan** — founder of **interpersonal theory of personality**; believed that mental disorders arise from disturbances in **interpersonal communication**.
4. **Erik Erikson** — developed the **psychosocial theory of personality development**, describing **eight stages**, each defined by a **social crisis** rather than a sexual one, as in Freud's theory.

12.2. The Core Idea of Neo-Freudianism

Personality is formed not only under the influence of **internal biological instincts**, but above all through **social interaction, culture, and life experience**.

12.3. The State of Contemporary Psychoanalysis and the Freudian Tradition in Ukraine

Figure 7. The International Institute of Depth Psychology, Kyiv.

The **National Psychological Association of Ukraine (NPA)**, through its division *"Psychoanalytic Psychology and Psychotherapy"*, unites practicing psychoanalysts and operates according to international standards. The **Ukrainian Psychoanalytic Union (UPU)** is an organization oriented toward psychoanalytic therapists and specialists, providing both a consultation center and a professional community.

The **Kyiv International School of Relational Psychoanalysis and Psychotherapy (KISRPP)**, founded in 2019, focuses on the **relational psychoanalytic tradition**, with a regional emphasis on Ukraine and Eastern Europe. The **International Institute of Depth Psychology (IIDP, Kyiv)** is a higher educational institution for training specialists in **psychoanalysis and depth psychology**.

The **Ukrainian Association for Transference-Focused Psychotherapy (TFP)** is a professional community that applies **psychoanalytically oriented methods**, particularly in working with **personality disorders**, in Ukraine.

Thus, there exists a **well-developed infrastructure** for psychoanalytic education and professional practice — including educational institutions, certification bodies, and organizations operating in line with **international standards**.

12.4. Historical and Theoretical Context

The history of psychoanalysis in Ukraine dates back to the **early 20th century**, when the ideas of **Sigmund Freud** were received by Ukrainian intellectuals and psychologists.

Although the **Soviet period** severely restricted the development of psychoanalysis as an independent discipline, after Ukraine's independence there began a **revival and institutionalization** of psychoanalytic practice.

In his theoretical work *"Oases of Psychoanalytic Discourse in Ukraine and the Personality of Sigmund Freud"*, **Anatolii Vasylovych Furman** emphasizes that psychoanalysis in Ukraine develops **not merely as a borrowed doctrine**, but as a phenomenon reflecting **specific cultural and historical conditions**.

12.5. Practice and Application

Psychoanalytic and psychoanalytically oriented therapy is available in Ukraine, both in **individual** and **group** formats. For example, therapists in Kyiv offer classical psychoanalysis and therapy in several languages. These services are aimed not only at general psychological well-being but also at working with **deep personality structures**, **traumas**, and **complex disorders**. The **Ukrainian Association for TFP** places special emphasis on the use of **psychoanalysis (or its modifications)** in treating individuals with **severe psychopathologies**.

12.6. Challenges and Specific Features of the Ukrainian Context

Cultural and historical heritage: Ukraine has unique cultural-historical factors influencing the perception of psychoanalysis (e.g., Soviet trauma, war, and post-Soviet transformations). Psychoanalysis in Ukraine often reflects not only **individual**, but also **collective and historical traumas**.

Institutionalization and standardization: One key challenge is the establishment of a **system of professional training and certification** that meets **international requirements** (e.g., those of the **International Psychoanalytical Association, IPA**).

Economic and resource limitations: Psychoanalytic methods often require **long-term therapy**, raising issues of **accessibility** for the general population.

Adequate application in trauma contexts: In the setting of **war and widespread trauma** (especially relevant for Ukraine), questions arise as to how well **classical psychoanalytic models** can be adapted to such conditions, and how they can be integrated with **crisis psychological interventions**.

Interpretation and adaptation of theory: Freud's ideas — the **unconscious, early childhood experiences, transference/countertransference** — require reinterpretation within the **Ukrainian cultural context** and in light of **contemporary research**, which is actively taking place.

12.7. Prospects

Growing interest in depth approaches: Both among professionals and the public, there is an increasing interest not only in **short-term therapeutic models**, but also in **deeper, analytic approaches**.

Education and international partnership: The number of **training programs, seminars, and international collaborations** (e.g., guest lectures by international analysts) is steadily increasing.

Expansion of professional communities and therapy accessibility: As psychoanalytic infrastructure develops, services are expected to become more **widely available**, with new **socially oriented programs** emerging.

Adaptation of methods to Ukrainian realities: The **historical and contemporary context** of Ukraine (war trauma, social transformation) necessitates the **adaptation of psychoanalytic methods**, potentially forming a **distinct niche** within **Ukrainian psychoanalytic practice**.

12.8. Borys Hryhorovych Khersonsky

In Ukraine, one of the most significant interpreters and cultural–philosophical popularizers of Freud's ideas in the post-Soviet space is **Borys Hryhorovych Khersonsky**.

Borys Hryhorovych Khersonsky (born 1950, Odesa) is a **Ukrainian psychiatrist, clinical psychologist, poet, essayist, and translator**, Doctor of Medical Sciences, and Professor.

He has been nominated for the **Joseph Conrad Literary Award** (granted by the Polish Institute in Kyiv), received the **International Literary Award "The Russian**

Prize" (second degree) for his book *"Before It Gets Dark"*, and was awarded the **Joseph Brodsky Fellowship (Grant-Award)** by the Joseph Brodsky Foundation in 2008.

He is one of the **key figures in the humanitarian and psychological culture** of Ukraine and the post-Soviet region, combining **psychoanalytic thinking** with **literary and philosophical approaches**.

His Attitude Toward Freudianism

Khersonsky is **not a direct follower** or academic continuator of Freud — he did not establish any new psychoanalytic schools.

However, he made a **significant contribution** to the **interpretation and adaptation** of psychoanalytic ideas within **Ukrainian psychology and the humanities**.

Main Areas of His Contribution:

1. **Popularization of Psychoanalysis**

Khersonsky wrote and lectured widely, explaining the ideas of **Freud, Jung, Fromm**, and other Western analysts to a broad audience.

He helped make psychoanalytic thinking **understandable and relevant** to the **Soviet and post-Soviet reader**.

2. **Psychoanalysis of Culture and Personality**

In his essays and poetry, he employs **psychoanalytic motifs** — themes of the **unconscious**, **trauma**, **memory**, **inner conflict**, **guilt**, and **love**.

3. **Critical Reflection on Freudianism**

Khersonsky was **not a dogmatist**. He saw Freud as a **foundational figure**, yet emphasized that Freud's ideas **require cultural and ethical reinterpretation** in the modern context.

4. **Synthesis of Psychoanalysis and Christian Tradition**

In his later works, Khersonsky sought to **integrate psychoanalytic views of the inner world** with **Christian anthropology** — a rare and complex approach that distinguishes him from classical psychoanalysts.

Thus, Borys Khersonsky is **not a reformer or scientific continuator** of Freud, but rather an **interpreter and humanistic popularizer**, who brought Freudian ideas into the context of **Ukrainian–Russian culture, poetry, and philosophy of personality**.

Examples of Khersonsky's Use of Psychoanalytic Ideas

1. **The Theme of Memory and Repression**

Many of Khersonsky's poems and essays center on **repressed memories, childhood traumas**, and the attempt to **comprehend them** — themes central to psychoanalysis.

"I remember all that I should not remember,

all that I should forget — I still recall."

This tone echoes Freud's notion that **the repressed never truly disappears**, but returns in symbolic form — through **dreams, slips of the tongue, creativity, or pain**.

Khersonsky poetically demonstrates how **the unconscious speaks** through **memory and emotion**.

2. **Psychoanalysis as a Path to Self-Knowledge**

In his essays and interviews, Khersonsky often says that **psychoanalysis is not merely therapy**, but a **path toward understanding oneself**. He wrote that in psychotherapy, a person faces their **inner "shadow"** — what they are unwilling to acknowledge within themselves.

"Psychoanalysis teaches responsibility for one's own unconscious. Not God, not parents, not the system — but you yourself are responsible for what lives within you."

This stance is close to **Erich Fromm's existential neo-Freudianism**, where the person is not a bundle of instincts, but a being capable of **self-knowledge and moral choice**.

3. **Religion and Psychoanalysis**

A deeply religious man, Khersonsky seeks to **reconcile psychoanalysis with Christian spirituality**.

He views psychoanalysis not as an **enemy of faith**, but as a **means to understand sin, guilt, repentance, and the divided nature of the self** more profoundly.

"Confession is also a form of psychoanalysis —

only addressed not to the therapist, but to God."

Here, he effectively merges Freud's **concept of the unconscious** with the **theological idea of conscience and spiritual struggle**.

4. **Intergenerational Trauma and the Collective Unconscious**

In his poems about **Odesa, the Holocaust, and Soviet experience**, Khersonsky explores **trauma transmitted across generations** — not only individual but **cultural and historical**.

He shows how **history penetrates the psyche**, shaping fear and guilt.

This idea parallels **Carl Jung's concept of the collective unconscious**, though Khersonsky expresses it in a **more human, psychological key**.

5. **Poetry as a Form of Psychoanalysis**

For Khersonsky, **poetry itself is therapy**.
He writes that poems **bring to light what cannot be said directly** — embodying Freud's principle:

"Where Id was, there shall Ego be."

Poetry becomes a **means of awareness and integration** of the unconscious.

Borys Khersonsky does not create a new psychoanalytic school,

but he achieves something **Freud himself could not** —

he unites **psychoanalysis, culture, memory, faith, and poetry**, creating a **holistic understanding of the human inner world**.

13. Transition to the Cognitive Paradigm: From Symbol to Process

The second half of the 20th century brought a radical rethinking of the concept of the psyche. With the development of cybernetics, information theory, and cognitive psychology, there was a shift from the psychodynamic metaphor to an information-processing paradigm.

J. Miller, U. Neisser, H. Simon, and others considered the psyche as an information-processing system, where consciousness and the unconscious represent different levels of cognitive processing.

Unconscious processes began to be understood not as repressed desires but as automatic computational procedures that ensure efficient thinking and adaptation (Reber, 1993; Kihlstrom, 1987).

In this context, Freud's concept of the unconscious underwent a transformation: symbolic conflict was replaced by an information filter—a mechanism of selective access to data for consciousness.

13.1. Cognitive Realism and Neurophilosophy

Modern philosophy of mind relies on the principles of cognitive realism—a perspective asserting that mental processes truly exist as neurophysiological structures and functions of the brain.

D. Dennett (1991) and P. Churchland (1995) rejected the dualism of consciousness and matter, arguing that "mental states are neural states described in another language."

In this paradigm, the unconscious acquires ontological reality, not as a "depth of the psyche," but as a level of neural integration preceding consciousness.

Dennett (1991): "Consciousness is not a place in the brain, but a process of competitive processing in which most events remain unconscious."

Cognitive realism unites Freud's idea of hidden activity with the physicalist understanding of the brain as a self-organizing information system.

We develop a philosophical interpretation of network neurophysiology, viewing the psyche as a topological hierarchy of functional systems, where the unconscious is a level of background-automatic network activity that ensures the continuity and coherence of conscious processes.

Consciousness does not arise from nothing: it is the product of self-organization of network activity, while the unconscious is a continuous field of neural dynamics forming the background for cognitive states.

The study of the unconscious becomes interdisciplinary—psychoanalysis, neuroscience, and cognitive science form a shared platform for describing psychic dynamics.

Unlike the Cartesian "I think," modern science considers the psyche as a system of network processes, where the subject is the result of interaction, not the cause.

Instead of interpreting symbols (as in Freud), neural network activity modeling and analysis of the topology of functional brain connections are used. If psychoanalysis was a hermeneutic science (understanding through interpretation), cognitive neuroscience is a reconstructive science (understanding through process simulation).

Recognizing that much human behavior is determined by unconscious neural processes leads to a reevaluation of concepts such as free will, responsibility, and subjective autonomy.

13.2. Synthesis: From the Freudian Subject to the Network Ontology of the Psyche

The modern stage in the development of the concept of the unconscious can be seen as a philosophical synthesis of three lines:

1. **Psychodynamic** (Freud, Jung, Adler)—where the unconscious acts as the energetic depth of personality;
2. **Cognitive** (Neisser, Kihlstrom, Damasio)—where it is understood as a level of automatic information processing;
3. **Network** (Lobasyuk, Tonni, Deaen)—where the unconscious becomes a topological structure supporting the stability of consciousness.

This synthesis represents a shift from an anthropocentric model of the psyche to a systemic one, in which humans are considered a complex cognitive network embedded in broader levels of the biosphere and society.

In conclusion, the concept of the unconscious has evolved from metaphor to model. For Freud, it was symbolic energy and conflict of the will; for cognitive scientists, it is an automatic level of information; for network neurophysiologists, it is the functional self-organization of the brain.

This evolution reflects a general shift in the philosophy of science: from metapsychology to cognitive realism, from interpretation of meaning to modeling dynamic systems.

Thus, modern philosophy of the unconscious combines Freudian depth, cognitive precision, and network ontology, forming a new understanding of humans as self-regulating systems of meaning, energy, and information.

13.3. Functions and Typology of the Unconscious in Modern Cognitive Science

Modern cognitive science views the unconscious not as a single phenomenon but as a multiple system of processes performing various functions in cognitive, emotional, and behavioral domains. The classical Freudian differentiation (unconscious, preconscious, consciousness) retains historical significance; however, it is now structured according to functional and neurophysiological characteristics, allowing integration of psychoanalytic, cognitive, and neurophysiological perspectives.

13.3.1. Emotional Unconscious

The emotional unconscious is associated with automatic processing of affective stimuli and regulation of behavior based on somatic markers (Damasio, 1999).

Functions:

Providing instantaneous emotional evaluation of stimuli;

Predicting potentially dangerous or beneficial situations;

Modeling behavior without conscious involvement.

Neurophysiological basis:

Amygdala, hippocampus, orbitofrontal cortex, insula;

Delta and theta rhythms in EEG correlated with automatic emotion processing (Sergent et al., 2005).

The emotional unconscious ensures adaptive behavioral efficiency, especially in stressful and dynamic situations.

13.3.2. Procedural Unconscious

The procedural unconscious is responsible for automated skills and actions formed through learning and experience.

Functions:

Enabling rapid execution of habitual actions (e.g., walking, writing, playing a musical instrument);

Minimizing cognitive load on consciousness;

Maintaining cognitive efficiency in complex and repetitive tasks.

Neurophysiological basis:

Basal ganglia, cerebellum, motor cortex;

Automatic patterns of network activity activated without conscious control.

The procedural unconscious is closely linked to the theory of learning through repetition and synaptic reinforcement, making it essential for skill and experience formation.

13.3.3. Cognitive Unconscious

The cognitive unconscious provides non-conscious information processing, including perception, attention, memory, and problem-solving.

Functions:

Processing large volumes of sensory information before it becomes available to consciousness;

Forming intuitive decisions based on probabilistic data integration;

Supporting creativity through automatic generation of alternative solutions.

Neurophysiological basis:

Associative cortical areas, preconscious-level neural networks;

Local activations that do not integrate into the global network of consciousness (Dehaene, 2014).

The cognitive unconscious forms the structural foundation of thought, allowing consciousness to focus on a limited number of significant elements.

13.3.4. Network Integration of Unconscious Processes

Modern network models (Lobasyuk, 2023) view the unconscious as a dynamic field of interacting processes, including emotional, procedural, and cognitive unconscious:

Each type of unconscious is represented by local neural circuits that can operate autonomously;

Consciousness emerges when these circuits undergo global integration;

The unconscious ensures system stability, predictability, and adaptability across diverse cognitive and behavioral tasks.

The unconscious is a functional architecture of the brain, providing continuity of cognitive activity and predictive modulation of conscious experience.

13.3.5. Practical Significance of the Typology

The typology of the unconscious has practical applications:

Psychotherapy and psychoanalysis: Differentiating emotional and cognitive unconscious aids in developing intervention strategies;

Learning and skill development: Procedural unconscious serves as a target for training programs;

Neuroscience and artificial intelligence: Cognitive unconscious allows modeling of automatic processes in neural network simulations.

Contemporary cognitive science treats the unconscious as a multi-functional level of the psyche, integrating emotional, procedural, and cognitive processes:

Emotional unconscious provides adaptive responses;

Procedural unconscious automates skills;

Cognitive unconscious enables preconscious information processing.

Network integration of these processes forms the basis of conscious experience, making the unconscious an integral part of the cognitive architecture of the individual.

13.4. The Unconscious: From Freud to the Network Cognitive Model

Introduction

The concept of the unconscious has evolved from Freud's metaphysical and psychodynamic idea to the modern network cognitive model, integrating psychoanalysis, cognitive science, and neurophysiology. This development reflects the shift from hermeneutic understanding of the psyche to formalized, experimentally testable models, where the unconscious is considered the functional foundation of consciousness.

13.4.1. Freudian Unconscious

Sigmund Freud (1915, 1920, 1933) defined the unconscious as:

A source of repressed desires and impulses;

A structure shaping personality and psychic conflicts;

A functional system operating independently of conscious control.

Key aspects:

Preconscious — a borderline level of information;

Consciousness — a narrow zone of accessible processes;

Repression — a mechanism preventing awareness of threatening desires.

Freud disrupted the notion of a transparent subject, establishing an epistemological foundation for the unconscious as a real, operative level of the psyche.

14. Lobasyuk B.A.'s Network Semantic-Topological Model of Consciousness

The Psyche as a Network of Meanings and Topologies

The title **"network semantic-topological method"** implies that the psyche can be analyzed as a network of meanings (semantics) and interrelations (topology). That is, not merely as a linear process "signal → processing → reaction," but as a multitude of interconnected elements, nodes, links, and configurations. Moreover, this method views the psyche as a network construct consisting of multiple interrelated networks.

At the foundation (basis) of mental activity undoubtedly lies a neural network construction that describes the rhythms of the electroencephalogram (EEG) as nodes and the relations between them as systems of connections. Figures 8–14 present polycyclic multigraphs reflecting the regression relationships between EEG rhythm amplitudes within a single pair of electrodes and within a single rhythm for right- and left-handed subjects in the left and right hemispheres; polycyclic multigraphs describing regression relationships between factor indicators of the Cattell and Eysenck tests for right- and left-handed subjects; and polycyclic multigraphs describing regression interrelations between factor indicators of V.M. Rusalov's OFDST questionnaire for right- and left-handed extroverts and introverts.

The relations were determined using multiple regression analysis, followed by geometric interpretation through polycyclic multigraphs.

Figures 8 and 9 present polycyclic multigraphs reflecting regression interrelations between EEG rhythm amplitudes within one pair of electrodes (A, B) and within a single rhythm (C, D) for right-handers (A, C) and left-handers (B, D) in the left (Figure 8) and right (Figure 9) hemispheres.

When calculating regression coefficients between EEG rhythm amplitudes within a single rhythm in left-handers, 1.16 times more regression coefficients were identified in the left hemisphere, and twice as many in the right hemisphere.

When calculating regression coefficients between EEG rhythm amplitudes within a single derivation but between different rhythms in left-handers, 1.4 times more regression coefficients were identified in the left hemisphere, and 2.25 times more in the right hemisphere.

Thus, both within a single EEG rhythm and within a single derivation between different rhythms, left-handers demonstrated a greater number of regression coefficients between EEG rhythm amplitudes than right-handers.

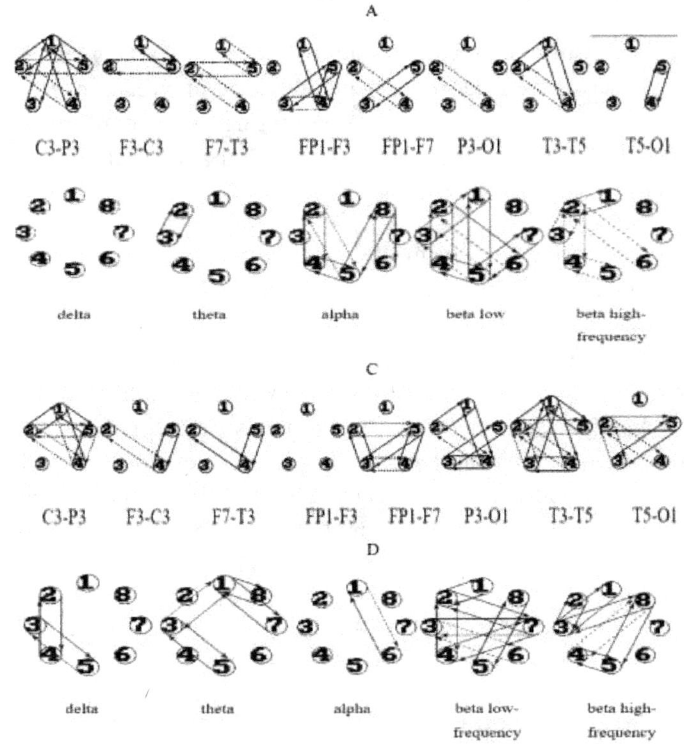

Figure 8. *Polycyclic multigraphs illustrating the relationships between EEG rhythm amplitudes within a single electrode pair (A, B) and within a single rhythm (C, D) in right-handed (A, C) and left-handed (B, D) individuals in the left hemisphere.*

Electrode pairs (A, B): C3–P3 – centro-parietal, F3–C3 – fronto-central, F7–T3 – temporo-central, FP1–F3 – frontal, FP1–F7 – fronto-temporal, P3–O1 – parieto-occipital, T3–T5 – posterior-temporal, T5–O1 – temporo-occipital.

EEG rhythms (C, D): Delta, theta, alpha, low-frequency beta, high-frequency beta.

Notes: Numbers in the nodes of graphs A and B indicate EEG rhythms; numbers in the nodes of graphs C and D indicate electrode pairs. Solid lines represent positive influences, while dashed lines indicate negative influences.

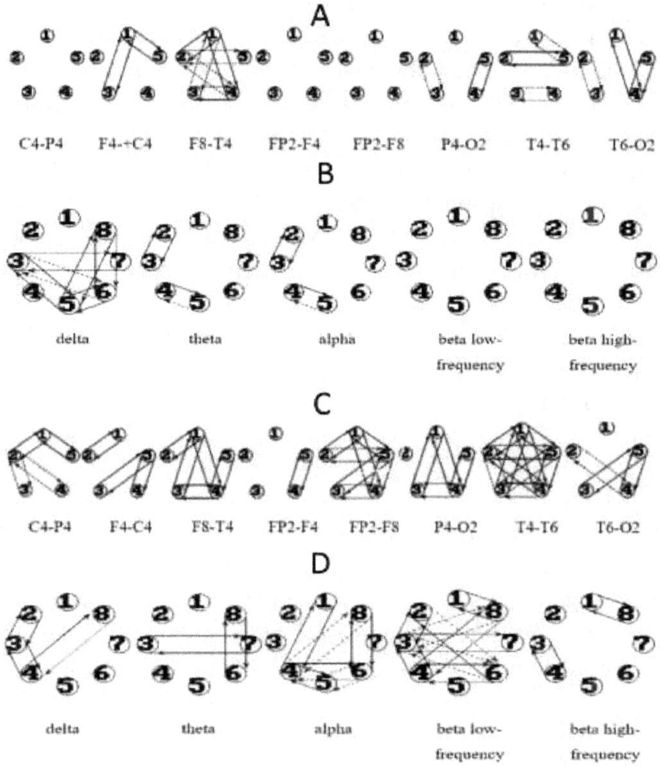

Figure 9. *Polycyclic multigraphs illustrating the relationships between EEG rhythm amplitudes within a single electrode pair (A, C) and within a single rhythm (B, D) in right-handed (A, B) and left-handed (C, D) individuals in the right hemisphere.*

Electrode pairs (A, C):

1 — C4–P4 (centro-parietal), 2 — F4–C4 (fronto-central), 3 — F8–T4 (temporo-central), 4 — FP2–F4 (frontal), 5 — FP2–F8 (fronto-temporal), 6 — P4–O2 (parieto-occipital), 7 — T4–T6 (posterior-temporal), 8 — T6–O2 (temporo-occipital).

EEG rhythms (B, D):

1 — delta, 2 — theta, 3 — alpha, 4 — low-frequency beta, 5 — high-frequency beta.

Notes: Numbers in the graph nodes indicate: in graphs A and B — EEG rhythms; in graphs C and D — electrode pairs.

It can be assumed that cortical tone is higher in left-handed individuals compared to right-handed ones. According to the views of V.S. Rusinov's school (1987), an increase in the number of correlation connections between different EEG components reflects a general increase in cortical tone, while a decrease indicates reduced tone.

In both left- and right-handed individuals, the highest number of relational connections in the left hemisphere within a single derivation was observed at C3–P3 (centro-parietal). This derivation may serve as a focal point for the influence of generators of different EEG rhythms in the left hemisphere.

In the right hemisphere, the highest number of relational connections in a single derivation for right-handed individuals was observed at F8–T4 (temporo-central), and for left-handed individuals at T4–T6 (posterior-temporal). This derivation may act as a focal point for the influence of EEG rhythm generators in the right hemisphere.

When calculating the number of regression coefficients in right-handed individuals within a single rhythm across different derivations in the left hemisphere, the highest number of coefficients was found in low- and high-frequency beta and alpha rhythms, and the lowest in delta and theta rhythms. In the right hemisphere, the pattern was opposite: the highest number of regression coefficients occurred in the delta rhythm, and the lowest in low- and high-frequency beta rhythms.

For left-handed individuals, when calculating the number of regression coefficients within a single rhythm across derivations in the left hemisphere, the highest number of regression relations was also in low- and high-frequency beta rhythms, and the lowest in the alpha rhythm. In the right hemisphere, the highest number of regression relations was in low-frequency beta, and the lowest in theta and high-frequency beta rhythms.

These results suggest that low- and high-frequency beta rhythms serve as controlling integrative rhythms of electrical activity in the left hemisphere of right-handed individuals and in both hemispheres of left-handed individuals. For right-handed individuals in the left hemisphere, the controlling integrative rhythm appears to be delta.

Based on the above, the structure of the electrical activity system can be assumed to be reticular, possessing topological properties.

Earlier, we conceptualized a unit of psychic activity as a psychological-psychiatric and neurophysiological construct formed based on multiple regression analysis of EEG parameters and the Lüscher anxiety test (Bitensky, V.S., Lobasyuk

B.A., Bodelan M.I., 2010). Considering the results obtained in this study, the unit of neurophysiological activity can be regarded as a regression relationship between EEG parameters.

Thus, the mathematical model of electrical activity we obtained can be classified as a labile, lattice-topological structure.

The next level of networked and hierarchical organization of the psyche involves the individual-typological features of personality.

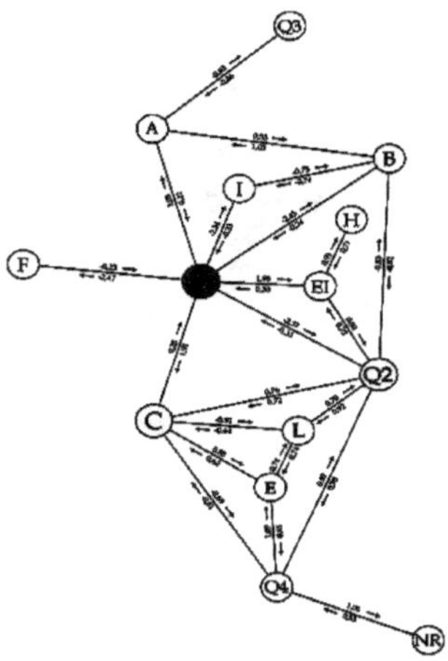

Figure 10. *Semantic network (polycyclic multigraph) illustrating regression relationships between Cattell and Eysenck test factors in right-handed participants.*

In the constructed semantic network describing regression relationships between the factor indicators of the Cattell and Eysenck tests in right-handed individuals, **Moral Normativity (Factor G)** appears to play the role of a controlling (system-forming) element.

In Cattell's model, Moral Normativity is a trait reflecting the strength of an individual's internal moral control—that is, the degree to which moral standards and a sense of responsibility are expressed.

It is not directly related to intelligence but pertains to the personality structure described through 16 factors.

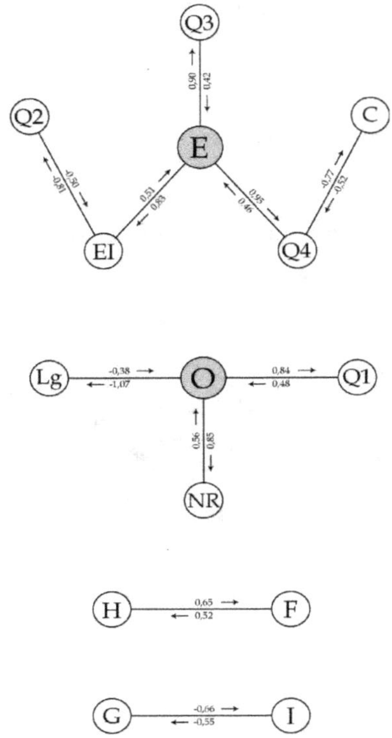

Figure 11. *Individual-personality construct (tree graph) describing the regression relationships between factor indicators of the Cattell and Eysenck tests in left-handed subjects.*

The identified regression relationships in left-handed individuals did not form a polycyclic multigraph, but only produced a fragmented tree graph consisting of four elements (Figure 11).

Since applying multiple linear regression did not yield a semantic network for left-handed subjects, we decided to use various linearization methods линеаризации ($y=x^2$, $y=x^3$, $y=x^4$, $y=sin(x)$, $y=cos(x)$, $y=log(x)$, $y=tg(x)$, $y=cotg(x)$).

It was found that linearizing the Cattell and Eysenck test indicators using the function y=x4y = x^4y=x4 allowed the construction of a coherent semantic network.

In this case, the number of regression relationships between test indicators increased from 20 to 34, while the number of statistically significant correlation coefficients decreased from 35 to 21. This indicates that, in left-handed individuals, the relationships between test indicators are more nonlinear than in right-handed individuals. The geometric interpretation of the multiple regression analysis of the linearized indicators allowed the construction of a semantic network (Figure 12).

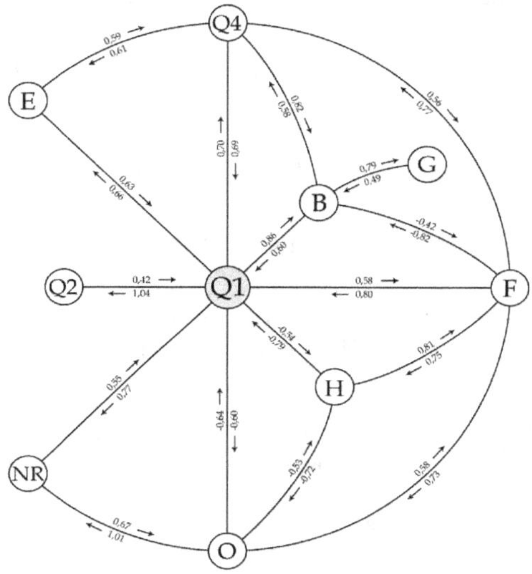

Figure 12. *Semantic network (polycyclic multigraph) describing the regression relationships between factor indicators of the Cattell and Eysenck tests in left-handed subjects, with test indicators linearized using the function Y=X4Y = X^4Y=X4.*

The results indicate that the internal regulatory mechanisms within the personality trait structure differ between right-handed and left-handed individuals. Literature on the study of regression relationships between EEG rhythm amplitudes in humans shows that an increase in regression relationships generally reflects higher cortical tone. Therefore, the greater number of regression relationships in right-handed individuals may indicate a higher level of tension in the regulatory mechanisms governing personality traits compared to left-handed individuals. In contrast, left-handed individuals exhibit greater nonlinearity in the regulatory mechanisms within the spatial structure of the psyche.

The OFDI methodology (Questionnaire of Formally-Dynamic Properties of Personality), developed by V. M. Rusalov (1979, 1986), is one of the most widely used tools in modern differential psychophysiology for studying temperament.

The methodology is based on the idea that temperament manifests not only in emotional reactions but also in the formally-dynamic characteristics of activity and communication. Rusalov identifies two main aspects of temperament expression:

1. **Object-activity aspect** – related to practical activities, task performance, and manipulation of objects;
2. **Communicative aspect** – related to interaction and communication with other people.

Diagnosed properties:

Each aspect is assessed according to four basic properties:

1. **Ergicity (energy)** – level of activity, performance capacity, endurance;
2. **Plasticity** – behavioral flexibility, ability to switch quickly between activities or modes of action;
3. **Tempo** – speed of performing actions or reactions;
4. **Emotionality** – degree of emotional excitability, impressionability, and sensitivity to events.

Interpretation:
The combination of these properties allows one to:

Quantitatively evaluate a person's temperamental traits;

Relate them to classical temperament types (choleric, sanguine, phlegmatic, melancholic);

Draw conclusions about adaptability, effectiveness, emotional stability, etc.

Applications:
The OFDI questionnaire is used in:

Psychological diagnostics (individual counseling, career guidance);

Personality research;

Professional psychology (assessing temperament suitability for job requirements).

Further interpretation:

Each factor reflects dynamic characteristics of temperament, not personality traits;

The profile allows evaluation of how stable, adaptive, quick, and emotionally stable a person is in different contexts—both instrumental (task-related) and social;

The questionnaire is often used in career guidance, psychophysiological studies, and psychological assessment of operators, athletes, military personnel, and others.

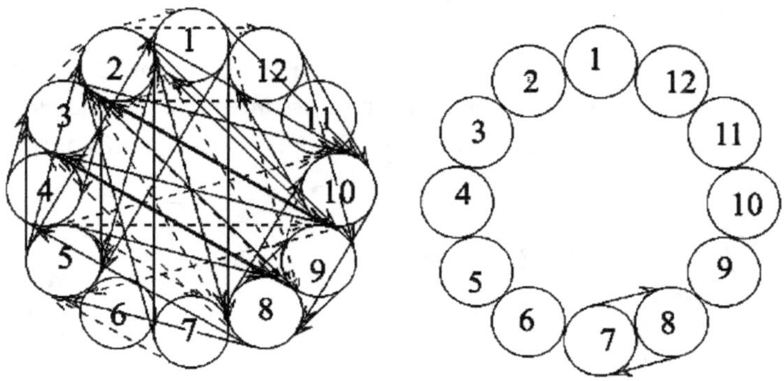

Figure 13. *Polycyclic multigraphs (semantic networks) describing the regression relationships between factor indicators of V.M. Rusalov's test (OFDST questionnaire) in right-handed (A) and left-handed (B) individuals.*

Legend:

1 — Psychomotor ergicity (ERM), 2 — Intellectual ergicity (ERI), 3 — Communicative ergicity (ERK), 4 — Psychomotor plasticity (PM), 5 — Intellectual plasticity (PI), 6 — Communicative plasticity (PK), 7 — Psychomotor tempo (SM)

8 — Intellectual tempo (SI), 9 — Communicative tempo (SK), 10 — Psychomotor emotionality (EM), 11 — Intellectual emotionality (EI), 12 — Communicative emotionality (EK)

The **Questionnaire of Formally-Dynamic Properties of Personality (OFDIS)** by V.M. Rusalov is used to assess characteristics of the motor (psychomotor) and intellectual (mental) domains, as well as the communicative (social) aspects of temperament.

According to S.L. Rubinstein, "temperament" is the dynamic aspect of personality, manifested in impulsivity and the pace of mental activity. Among individual characteristics that strongly influence behavior, temperament occupies a significant place. It is one of the most stable traits, as it has a genetic basis, meaning that individual features of temperament are innate.

A greater number of connections—linear regression dependencies—were identified in right-handed individuals compared to left-handed individuals, which may indicate a higher tension of regulatory mechanisms that support the object-activity and communicative aspects of temperament in right-handers. This also suggests that the system of formally-dynamic properties of personality in right-handers is more rigidly organized and less variable than in left-handers.

Considering that the highest number of connections was found with the indicator of intellectual ergicity in right-handers, it can be assumed that this indicator serves as a system-forming characteristic of their formally-dynamic properties of personality.

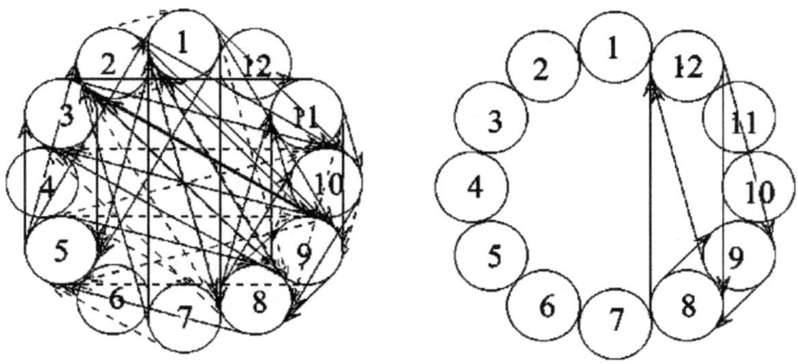

Figure 14. *Polycyclic multigraphs (semantic networks) describing the regression relationships between the factor indicators of V.M. Rusalov's test (OFDIS questionnaire) in* ***extraverts (A)*** *and* ***introverts (B)****.*

Legend: *same as in Figure 13.*

A greater number of connections — linear regression dependencies — was found in **extraverts** compared to **introverts**, which may indicate a higher level of tension in the regulatory mechanisms supporting the **object-activity** and **communicative** aspects of temperament in extraverts. This also suggests that the system of **formal-dynamic properties of individuality** in extraverts is more rigidly organized and less variable than in left-handers and introverts.

Since extraverts demonstrated **seven regression connections** each for *intellectual plasticity*, *intellectual tempo*, *communicative tempo*, and *psychomotor emotionality*, it can be assumed that these indicators play a particularly important role for extraverts in forming the systemic organization of the object-activity and communicative aspects of their temperament.

At the same time, no regression connections were found in extraverts for *psychomotor plasticity*, *communicative plasticity*, or *communicative emotionality*. This may indicate that these indicators are **non-systemic** within the structure of the object-activity and communicative aspects of temperament in extraverts.

14.1. The Network Nature of Mental Activity: Review of Modern Approaches and Research (2007–2025)

Modern psychology and neuroscience are gradually moving away from linear models of mental activity and striving to use more complex and integrative approaches that reflect the interconnected nature of mental processes. One such approach is **network analysis**, which allows the modeling of the psyche as a system of interconnected elements.

14.2. Network Analysis

Borsboom D. (2017), as well as later work by Borsboom D. and Cramer A.O.J. (2019), describe the methodology for constructing psychological networks, where nodes represent variables or symptoms and edges represent correlations or causal influences. Methods for evaluating network reliability and accuracy are discussed in detail.

Epskamp S. and Fried E.I. (2018) demonstrate the application of network analysis to the study of cognitive and emotional processes, highlighting the identification of central nodes and key connections within psychological structures.

Bringmann L.F., et al. (2015) examine the application of network models in clinical psychology, describing both structural symptom networks of mental disorders and dynamic changes in these networks.

Fried E.I., et al. (2021) use networks to describe relationships between personality traits and functional brain networks, offering an integrative view of individual differences.

Christensen A.P., Golino H.F., and Epskamp S. (2023) demonstrate the use of network analysis for cognitive, personality, and mental measures, revealing complex interconnections among them.

Cramer A.O.J., et al. (2010) show how various mental disorders can be considered as interconnected networks of symptoms rather than independent diagnoses.

Pajevic S. and Plenz D. (2012) studied neural networks underlying cognitive processes, emphasizing that the structural and functional network organization of the brain forms the basis of mental activity.

Smith L., et al. (2017) showed that network models of cognitive development demonstrate how a child's abilities form as interconnected elements of a network, with learning and development reflected in changes to network structure.

Lobasyuk B.A. and Bodelan M.I. (2015) proposed a method describing the psyche as a semantic network of individual-typological traits, identifying system-forming factors and the relationships between elements of the mental structure.

14.3. Key Principles of the Network Semantic-Topological Method

The **concept of network consciousness**, developed by us, is based on the **network semantic-topological method** and represents an innovative approach to understanding human consciousness through the lens of network structures and processes.

Unlike traditional models that treat consciousness as a centralized process, we propose viewing it as a **dynamic and decentralized network** of interacting elements.

14.4. Fundamental Principles of the Concept of Network Consciousness

1. **Decentralized Structure:**

   Consciousness is not a single center but a network of interacting elements, each contributing to the overall process.

2. **Dynamism and Variability:**

   Network consciousness is constantly changing, adapting to new conditions and information, allowing humans to respond effectively to changes in the environment.

3. **Interactivity:**
   Elements of the consciousness network interact with each other, exchanging information and experience, which facilitates learning and development.
4. **Collective Aspect:**

Network consciousness includes not only individual experience but also collective experience, reflecting the influence of social interactions on the formation of consciousness.

The concept of network consciousness resonates with the ideas of the **network paradigm** proposed by **Gregory Bateson**.

The network paradigm views the world as an open and decentralized system of interactions, emphasizing relationships between elements rather than the elements themselves.

This is consistent with our approach, which sees consciousness as a network of interacting elements where the key factor is not the elements themselves, but their **relations and interconnections**.

The concept of network consciousness represents a **modern and multifaceted approach** to understanding human consciousness, taking into account its complexity, dynamism, and social conditioning.

In our proposed model, the interaction between **electrogenesis**, **personality structure**, and **the formation of consciousness** is realized through a dynamic network of neural connections, where each element (a neuron or a neuronal group) plays a role in the formation of personal identity and consciousness.

14.5. Electrogenesis as the Basis of Neural Activity

In the context of neuropsychology, **electrogenesis** refers to the processes of generating electrical impulses by neurons, which form the basis of their functioning. These impulses enable information transmission between neurons, forming **neural networks** that underlie all mental processes, including **perception, memory, and consciousness**.

14.6. Personality Structure Through the Lens of Network Consciousness

In our concept, **personality** is viewed as a set of interconnected neural structures, each responsible for specific aspects of behavior, emotion, and cognitive function.

These structures are formed and modified through interaction with the environment, reflecting the **dynamic nature of personality**.

14.7. The Formation of Consciousness in the Network Model

We propose that **consciousness arises from the interaction of various neural networks** that process and integrate information into a coherent, conscious experience.

This interaction involves both **automatic and controlled processes**, allowing the individual to adapt to changes in both the external environment and internal state.

14.8. Interaction of Elements

Thus, **electrogenesis** provides the physical basis of neural activity; the **structure of personality** represents the organization of these neural networks; and **consciousness** emerges as the result of their interaction.

This interaction enables adaptation, learning, and development—key aspects of the proposed concept of **network consciousness**.

Modern cognitive science increasingly demonstrates a shift from **linear models of mental activity** to **network paradigms**, where consciousness is understood as the result of interactions among multiple neural and functional subsystems.

In this context, the concept developed by **B.A. Lobasyuk** occupies a distinctive place in contemporary **neurophysiology and cognitive science**.

Consciousness is proposed to be understood as a **network form of organization of brain activity**, where the key parameters are **connection topology, information integration, and self-organization of neural ensembles** (Lobasyuk, 2023).

In our view, consciousness cannot be reduced to the activity of isolated centers or modules; it is a **systemic-network process** that unites the brain's functional structures into a single **dynamic network**.

Thus, the proposed concept develops and generalizes the ideas of **P.K. Anokhin's systemic physiology, N.A. Bernstein's concept of functional systems**, and **network theories of cognitive processes**, providing a unified **neurophysiological basis for understanding consciousness**.

At the core of the network principle of consciousness organization lies the idea that consciousness represents a **multi-level, self-organizing network** that integrates sensory, associative, motor, and limbic cortical zones, as well as subcortical structures.

Consciousness arises not as a static structure but as a **dynamic configuration of connections** that ensures coherence between various brain regions. These processes can be described in terms of **network topology, nodal ensembles, and interhemispheric synchronization**.

Consciousness is a **neural-network form of reflection**, where **phase synchrony and coherence of oscillatory processes** serve as the physiological foundation of conscious experience.

It should be emphasized that **the coherence of electrical activity between the hemispheres** serves as an objective physiological indicator of conscious states — a fact confirmed by a series of **ECoG studies** (Lobasyuk, et al.).

One of the key experimental directions in understanding the mechanisms of consciousness is the **analysis of interhemispheric asymmetry coefficients (IAC)** of ECoG rhythms.

This analysis has shown that the **level of awareness directly correlates with the nature of interhemispheric interactions**.

It can thus be argued that **consciousness arises at the boundary of hemispheric integration**, where functional systems acquire the property of **network interconnectivity**.

14.9. The Cognitological Level of the Network Model

Consciousness functions not only as a **physiological network** but also as a **cognitive-semantic system** capable of integrating meanings. Here, consciousness is understood as a **network mechanism of semantic organization of experience**, where each element of cognitive content is distributed across multiple neural connections.

Meanings are not localized in specific brain regions; rather, they represent **topological fields** that emerge from the interaction of neuronal ensembles.

The integration of **neurophysiological** and **semiotic** levels of analysis makes the proposed concept a unique attempt to provide a **natural-scientific description of the phenomenology of consciousness**.

In the work *"The Semantic-Topological Model of Electrogenesis"* (Lobasyuk B.A. et al.), the nervous system and brain are considered not as a simple **stimulus–**

response chain, but as a **functionally organized network complex** characterized by **asymmetry**, **hemispheric specialization**, and **functional distribution**. This allows us to assert that the **psyche is inseparable from the brain's network organization** and is, in essence, an **informational network**.

In modern psychology, **network models**—such as **symptom networks** or **networks of cognitive processes**—are becoming increasingly popular, and the psyche is now viewed from the perspective of **information and network theories**.

If the psyche is a **network**, its nodes may represent:

— neuronal groups,

— functional zones,

— semantic constructs,

— linguistic signs,

— or subjective experiences.

Connections between them correspond to **information exchange**, **activation**, or **semantic flows**.

Such an approach makes it possible to account for the **complexity of the psyche**—its multiplicity of elements, nonlinearity, interdependence, and dynamism.

Within this concept, the **unconscious** ceases to be the "depth" of the psyche and becomes a **network foundation of cognitive ontology**—a **semantic substrate** of the brain that ensures its capacity for adaptive information processing.

Thus, the **philosophy of the network psyche** unites **Freudian phenomenology** with **cognitive realism** and **evolutionary neurophysiology**.

In the **network approach** (Lobasyuk, Tononi, Dehaene), the **unconscious** is interpreted as a **topological structure** that supports the **stability of consciousness**. This synthesis marks a transition from an **anthropocentric model of the psyche** to a **systemic one**, where the human being is viewed as a **complex cognitive network** embedded within broader levels of the **biosphere** and **society**.

Thus, the *"method of network semantic-topological analysis of psychological research results,"* based on **multidimensional evaluation**, **system analysis**, and the

construction of a conceptual semantic network visualizing the **architecture of regulation of individual-typological personality traits** and the **identification of system-forming factors of this network**, undoubtedly enables the revelation of the **essential mechanisms of mental activity**.

Literatura

1. Анохин П.К. *Философские аспекты теории функциональных систем.* — М.: Наука, 1978.
2. Анохин, П.К. *Биология и нейрофизиология условного рефлекса*. — М.: Медицина, 1975.
3. Артеменков В.В. Сетевое моделирование психологических конструктов. *Московский психологический журнал*, 2017.
4. Бернштейн, Н.А. *О построении движений*. — М.: Медгиз, 1947.
5. Гуссерль Э. *Идеи к чистой феноменологии*. — 1913.
6. Иванов В. (2021). *Нейронные корреляты сознания.* СПб.: Питер.
7. Ковальчук Т.М., et al. (2019). *Функциональные сети мозга и когнитивные процессы.* Киев: Научная мысль.
8. Кузнецов О.В. (2022). *Нейрофизиология сознания.* Киев: Наук. думка.
9. Лобасюк Б.А. (2010). *Системные нейрофизиологические механизмы электрогенеза головного мозга.* Одесса: ХГЭУ.
10. Лобасюк Б.А. (2018). *Сетевая нейрофизиология.* Одесса: ХГЭУ. – Развивает системно-сетевой подход к сознанию, интегрирующий физиологию и когнитивные процессы.
11. Лобасюк Б.А. *Естественно-научные основы психологии.* — Одесса: ХГЭУ, 2022. — 236 с.
12. Лобасюк Б.А. *Когнитология.* — Одесса: ХГЭУ, 2024. — 312 с.
13. Лобасюк Б.А. *Сетевая нейрофизиология.* — Одесса: ХГЭУ, 2023. — 284 с.
14. Лобасюк Б.А., Боделан М.И. Сетевой семантико-топологический метод в психологии. Одесса, 2015.
15. Мерло-Понти М. *Феноменология восприятия*. — 1945.
16. Тонни Дж. *Consciousness as Integrated Information. — Biological Bulletin*, 2008, 215(3): 216–242.
17. Фрейд З. *Лекции по введению в психоанализ*. — 1917.
18. Фрейд З. *Недовольство культурой*. — Вена, 1930.
19. Фрейд З. *По ту сторону принципа удовольствия*. — 1920.
20. Фрейд З. *Тотем и табу*. — Вена, 1913.
21. Фрейд З. *Я и Оно*. — Вена, 1923.
22. Фрейд, 3. *Введение в психоанализ*. — М.: Наука, 1991 (ориг. 1917).
23. Фрейд, 3. *Толкование сновидений*. — СПб.: Азбука-Классика, 2006 (ориг. 1900).
24. Фрейд, 3. *Я и Оно*. — М.: Наука, 1991 (ориг. 1923).
25. Чалмерс Д. (2013). *Сознающий ум: в поисках фундаментальной теории.* М.: Идея-Пресс.

26. Baars B.J. *A Cognitive Theory of Consciousness.* — Cambridge: CUP, 1988.
27. Bargh, J.A., Morsella, E. *The Unconscious Mind. // Perspectives on Psychological Science*, 2008, Vol. 3(1), p. 73–79.
28. Block, N. (1995). *On a confusion about a function of consciousness.* Behavioral and Brain Sciences, 18(2), 227–247.
29. Borsboom D. (2017). Estimating psychological networks and their accuracy: A tutorial paper.
30. Borsboom D. Estimating psychological networks and their accuracy: A tutorial paper. *Behavior Research Methods*, 2017.
31. Borsboom D., Cramer A. O. J. (2019). The network approach to psychopathology: a review of the literature 2008–2018.
32. Borsboom D., Cramer A.O.J., Kalis A. The network structure of mental disorders: A novel approach to understanding comorbidity. *Journal of Abnormal Psychology*, 2011.
33. Bringmann L.F., et al. Network analysis in clinical psychology. *Journal of Abnormal Psychology*, 2015.
34. Bugnyar, T. (2011). *Social Cognition in Corvids.* Comparative Cognition & Behavior Reviews, 6, 25–36.
35. Chalmers, D. *The Conscious Mind: In Search of a Fundamental Theory.* — Oxford: OUP, 1996.
36. Christensen A.P., Golino H.F., Epskamp S. Architecture and relationships among cognition, mental health and other human domains revealed by network analysis perspective. *Current Psychology*, 2023.
37. Churchland, P. *The Engine of Reason, the Seat of the Soul.* — MIT Press, 1995.
38. Cramer A.O.J., et al. (2010). Comorbidity: a network perspective.
39. Cramer A.O.J., et al. Comorbidity: a network perspective. *Behavioral and Brain Sciences*, 2010.
40. Crick, F. & Koch, C. (1990). Towards a Neurobiological Theory of Consciousness. Seminars in the Neurosciences, 2, 263–275. Buckner, R. L., Andrews-Hanna, J. R., Schacter, D. L. (2008). The Brain's Default Network. Annals of the NY Academy of Sciences, 1124, 1–38. Gallup, G. G. (1970). Chimpanzees: Self-Recognition. Science, 167, 86–87. Damasio, A. *Self Comes to Mind: Constructing the Conscious Brain.* — New York: Pantheon, 2010.
41. Damasio, A. *The Feeling of What Happens: Body and Emotion in the Making of Consciousness.* — New York: Harcourt, 1999.
42. Dehaene, S. & Naccache, L. (2001). *Towards a Cognitive Neuroscience of Consciousness: Basic Evidence and a Workspace Framework.* Cognition, 79, 1–37.

Edelman, G. M. (2004). *Wider than the Sky: The Phenomenal Gift of Consciousness.* Yale University Press.
Dehaene, S. (2014). *Consciousness and the Brain.* Viking.
Лобасюк, Б.А. (2015). *Сетевая нейрофизиология.* Одесса: ХГЭУ.
Llinás, R. R. (2001). *I of the Vortex: From Neurons to Self.* MIT Press.
Steriade, M. (1996). *Arousal: Re-Examining the Reticular Activating System.* Science, 272, 225–227.

43. Dehaene, S. (2014). *Consciousness and the Brain: Deciphering How the Brain Codes Our Thoughts.* Penguin.
44. Dehaene, S. *Consciousness and the Brain: Deciphering How the Brain Codes Our Thoughts*. — New York: Viking, 2014.
45. Dehaene, S., & Changeux, J. P. (2011). *Experimental and theoretical approaches to conscious processing.* Neuron, 70(2), 200–227.
46. Dehaene, S., Naccache, L. *Towards a cognitive neuroscience of consciousness: basic evidence and a workspace framework.* Cognition, 2001.
47. Dennett, D. *Consciousness Explained.* — Boston: Little, Brown, 1991.
48. Edelman, G. M. & Tononi, G. (2000). *A Universe of Consciousness: Ho*
49. Engel, A. K., & Singer, W. (2001). *Temporal binding and the neural correlates of sensory awareness.* Trends in Cognitive Sciences, 5(1), 16–25.
50. Epskamp S., Fried E.I. (2018). Psychological network analysis.
51. Epskamp S., Fried E.I. Psychological network analysis. *Annual Review of Clinical Psychology*, 2018.
52. Freud, S. *New Introductory Lectures on Psychoanalysis*. — New York: Norton, 1933.
53. Freud, S. *The Ego and the Id* (1923).
54. Freud, S. *The Unconscious* (1915) // Standard Edition, Vol. XIV. London: Hogarth Press, 1957.
55. Freud, S. *The Unconscious*. — London: Hogarth Press, 1915.
56. Fried E.I., et al. (2021). Personality network neuroscience: Promises and challenges on the way toward a unifying framework of individual variability. Christensen A.P., Golino H.F., Epskamp S. (2023). Architecture and relationships among cognition, mental health and other human domains +revealed by network analysis perspective. Cramer A.O.J., et al. (2010). Comorbidity: a network perspective.
57. Fried E.I., et al. Personality network neuroscience: Promises and challenges. *Network Neuroscience*, 2021.
58. Friston, K. (2019). *The Free Energy Principle: A Unified Brain Theory? Nature Reviews Neuroscience*, 11(2), 127–138.

59. Graziano, M. S. A. (2019). *Rethinking Consciousness: A Scientific Theory of Subjective Experience.* W.W. Norton.
60. Green, A. *The Fabric of Affect in the Psychoanalytic Discourse*. — London: Routledge, 2003.
61. Hameroff, S., Penrose, R. (2014). *Consciousness in the Universe: A Review of the 'Orch OR' Theory. Physics of Life Reviews*, 11(1), 39–78.
62. Kihlstrom, J. F. "The Cognitive Unconscious." *Science*, 237, 1987, pp. 1445–1452.
63. Kihlstrom, J.F. *The Cognitive Unconscious*. // *Science*, 1987, 237, pp. 1445–1452.
64. Koch, C., Massimini, M., Boly, M., & Tononi, G. (2016). *Neural correlates of consciousness: progress and problems.* Nature Reviews Neuroscience, 17, 307–321.
65. Kossakowski J.J., et al. (2024). A psychological network analysis of the relationship among component importance measures.
66. LeDoux, J. *The Emotional Brain*. — New York: Simon & Schuster, 1996.
67. Libet, B. *Unconscious cerebral initiative and the role of conscious will in voluntary action*. Behavioral and Brain Sciences, 1985.
68. Lobasyuk B.A., Zamkova A.V., Bodelan M.I. *Network Semantic-Topological Model of Electrogenesis. // Journal of Cognitive and Systems Neuroscience.* — 2024. — Vol. 5(2). — P. 55–72.
69. Lobasyuk, B. A. *Network Semantic-Topological Model of Electrogenesis*. // *Psychology and Neuroscience*, 2024.
70. Lobasyuk, B. A. *Network Semantic-Topological Model of Electrogenesis*. // *Psychology and Neuroscience*, 2024.
71. Lobasyuk, B.A. *Network Neurophysiology*. — Odesa: HSEU Press, 2023.
72. Lobasyuk, B.A. *Network Semantic-Topological Model of Electrogenesis*. // *Psychology and Neuroscience*, 2024.
73. Lobasyuk, B.A., Bodelan, M.I., Zamkova, A.V. *Network Semantic-Topological Method in Psychology*. — Odesa, 2025.
74. Lobasyuk, B.A., Bodelan, M.I., Zamkova, A.V. *Network Semantic-Topological Method in Psychology*. — Odesa, 2025.
75. Lobasyuk, B.A., Bodelan, M.I., Zamkova, A.V. *Network Semantic-Topological Met*
76. Lobasyuk, B.A., Bodelan, M.I., Zamkova, A.V. *Сетевой семантико-топологический метод в психологии*. — Одесса, 2025.
77. Lobasyuk, B.A., Bodelan, M.I., Zamkova, A.V. *Сетевой семантико-топологический метод в психологии*. — Одесса, 2025.

78. Mashour, G. A., Roelfsema, P., Changeux, J.-P., Dehaene, S. (2020). *Conscious Processing and the Global Neuronal Workspace Hypothesis. Neuron*, 105(5), 776–798.
79. Michell L., et al. Psychological Network Analysis of General Self-Efficacy in High vs. Low Resilient Functioning Healthy Adults. *Frontiers in Psychiatry*, 2021.
80. Nietzsche, F. *Jenseits von Gut und Böse*. — Leipzig, 1886.
81. Northoff, G., Heinzel, A., de Greck, M., Bermpohl, F., Dobrowolny, H., & Panksepp, J. (2006). *Self-referential processing in our brain – a meta-analysis of imaging studies on the self.* NeuroImage, 31(1), 440–457.
82. Pajevic S., Plenz D. (2012). Neurocognitive networks: findings, models, and theory.
83. Panksepp, J. (1998). *Affective Neuroscience.* Oxford University Press. Plotnik, J. M., de Waal, F. B. M., Reiss, D. (2006). *Self-recognition in an Asian Elephant.* PNAS, 103, 17053–17057.
84. Panksepp, J. *Affective Neuroscience: The Foundations of Human and Animal Emotions*. — New York: Oxford Univ. Press, 1998.
85. Premack, D., & Woodruff, G. (1978). *Does the chimpanzee have a theory of mind?* Behavioral and Brain Sciences, 1(4), 515–526.
86. Pribram K. *Languages of the Brain.* — Monterey, 1971.
87. Raichle, M. E. et al. *A Default Mode of Brain Function // PNAS*, 2001. Vol. 98 (2), p. 676–682.
88. Reber, A. *Implicit Learning and Tacit Knowledge*. — Oxford University Press, 1993.
89. Rosenthal, D. M. (2005). *Consciousness and Mind.* Oxford University Press.
90. Schopenhauer, A. *Die Welt als Wille und Vorstellung*. — Leipzig, 1819.
91. Sergent, C., Baillet, S., Dehaene, S. *Timing of the brain events underlying access to consciousness during the attentional blink. Nature Neuroscience*, 2005.
92. Sergent, C., Baillet, S., Dehaene, S. *Timing of the brain events underlying access to consciousness during the attentional blink. Nature Neuroscience*, 2005.
93. Seth, A. (2021). *Being You: A New Science of Consciousness.* Faber & Faber.
94. Seth, A. *Being You: A New Science of Consciousness*. — London: Faber & Faber, 2021.
95. Shen X., et al. The network and interactive pattern of social adjustment and psychological symptoms in patients with spinal cord injury. *BMC Psychology*, 2025.
96. Shettleworth, S.J. *Cognition, Evolution, and Behavior*. — Oxford University Press, 2010.

97.Smith L., et al. (2017). Network Models for Cognitive Development and Intelligence.

Pajevic S., Plenz D. Neurocognitive networks: findings, models, and theory. *Trends in Cognitive Sciences*, 2012.

98.Smith L., et al. (2017). Network Models for Cognitive Development and Intelligence.

99.Smith L., et al. Network Models for Cognitive Development and Intelligence. *Journal of Intelligence*, 2017.

100. Smith, J. D., Shields, W. E., Washburn, D. A. (1995). Metacognition in Rhesus Monkeys. Cognition, 77, 23–41.

101. Tononi, G. (2004). *An information integration theory of consciousness.* BMC Neuroscience, 5, 42.

102. Tononi, G. (2008). *Consciousness as Integrated Information: A Provisional Manifesto. Biological Bulletin*, 215(3), 216–242.

103. Tononi, G. *An Information Integration Theory of Consciousness* (2008).

104. Tononi, G. *An Information Integration Theory of Consciousness*. — BMC Neuroscience, 2008.

105. Tononi, G. *An Information Integration Theory of Consciousness. BMC Neuroscience*, 2008.

106. Tononi, G., Koch, C. (2015). *Consciousness: Here, There and Everywhere? Philosophical Transactions of the Royal Society B*, 370(1668).

Literatura

1. Anohin P.K. Filosofskie aspekty teorii funkcionalnyh sistem. — M.: Nauka, 1978.
2. Anohin, P.K. Biologiya i nejrofiziologiya uslovnogo refleksa. — M.: Medicina, 1975.
3. Artemenkov V.V. Setevoe modelirovanie psihologicheskih konstruktov. Moskovskij psihologicheskij zhurnal, 2017.
4. Bernshtejn, N.A. O postroenii dvizhenij. — M.: Medgiz, 1947.
5. Gusserl E. Idei k chistoj fenomenologii. — 1913.
6. Ivanov V. (2021). Nejronnye korrelyaty soznaniya. SPb.: Piter.
7. Kovalchuk T.M., et al. (2019). Funkcionalnye seti mozga i kognitivnye processy. Kiev: Nauchnaya mysl.
8. Kuznecov O.V. (2022). Nejrofiziologiya soznaniya. Kiev: Nauk. dumka.
9. Lobasyuk B.A. (2010). Sistemnye nejrofiziologicheskie mehanizmy elektrogeneza golovnogo mozga. Odessa: HGEU.
10. Lobasyuk B.A. (2018). Setevaya nejrofiziologiya. Odessa: HGEU. – Razvivaet sistemno-setevoj podhod k soznaniyu, integriruyushij fiziologiyu i kognitivnye processy.
11. Lobasyuk B.A. Estestvenno-nauchnye osnovy psihologii. — Odessa: HGEU, 2022. — 236 s.
12. Lobasyuk B.A. Kognitologiya. — Odessa: HGEU, 2024. — 312 s.
13. Lobasyuk B.A. Setevaya nejrofiziologiya. — Odessa: HGEU, 2023. — 284 s.
14. Lobasyuk B.A., Bodelan M.I. Setevoj semantiko topologicheskij metod v psihologii. Odessa, 2015.
15. Merlo-Ponti M. Fenomenologiya vospriyatiya. — 1945.
16. Tonni Dzh. Consciousness as Integrated Information. — Biological Bulletin, 2008, 215(3): 216–242.
17. Frejd Z. Lekcii po vvedeniyu v psihoanaliz. — 1917.
18. Frejd Z. Nedovolstvo kulturoj. — Vena, 1930.
19. Frejd Z. Po tu storonu principa udovolstviya. — 1920.
20. Frejd Z. Totem i tabu. — Vena, 1913.
21. Frejd Z. Ya i Ono. — Vena, 1923.
22. Frejd, 3. Vvedenie v psihoanaliz. — M.: Nauka, 1991 (orig. 1917).
23. Frejd, 3. Tolkovanie snovidenij. — SPb.: Azbuka-Klassika, 2006 (orig. 1900).
24. Frejd, 3. Ya i Ono. — M.: Nauka, 1991 (orig. 1923).

25. Chalmers D. (2013). Soznayushij um: v poiskah fundamentalnoj teorii. M.: Ideya-Press.

26. Baars B.J. A Cognitive Theory of Consciousness. — Cambridge: CUP, 1988.

27. Bargh, J.A., Morsella, E. The Unconscious Mind. // Perspectives on Psychological Science, 2008, Vol. 3(1), p. 73–79.

28. Block, N. (1995). On a confusion about a function of consciousness. Behavioral and Brain Sciences, 18(2), 227–247.

29. Borsboom D. (2017). Estimating psychological networks and their accuracy: A tutorial paper.

30. Borsboom D. Estimating psychological networks and their accuracy: A tutorial paper. Behavior Research Methods, 2017.

31. Borsboom D., Cramer A. O. J. (2019). The network approach to psychopathology: a review of the literature 2008–2018.

32. Borsboom D., Cramer A.O.J., Kalis A. The network structure of mental disorders: A novel approach to understanding comorbidity. Journal of Abnormal Psychology, 2011.

33. Bringmann L.F., et al. Network analysis in clinical psychology. Journal of Abnormal Psychology, 2015.

34. Bugnyar, T. (2011). Social Cognition in Corvids. Comparative Cognition & Behavior Reviews, 6, 25–36.

35. Chalmers, D. The Conscious Mind: In Search of a Fundamental Theory. — Oxford: OUP, 1996.

36. Christensen A.P., Golino H.F., Epskamp S. Architecture and relationships among cognition, mental health and other human domains revealed by network analysis perspective. Current Psychology, 2023.

37. Churchland, P. The Engine of Reason, the Seat of the Soul. — MIT Press, 1995.

38. Cramer A.O.J., et al. (2010). Comorbidity: a network perspective.

39. Cramer A.O.J., et al. Comorbidity: a network perspective. Behavioral and Brain Sciences, 2010.

40. Crick, F. & Koch, C. (1990). Towards a Neurobiological Theory of Consciousness. Seminars in the Neurosciences, 2, 263–275.

Buckner, R. L., Andrews-Hanna, J. R., Schacter, D. L. (2008). The Brain's Default Network. Annals of the NY Academy of Sciences, 1124, 1–38.

Gallup, G. G. (1970). Chimpanzees: Self-Recognition. Science, 167, 86–87.

41. Damasio, A. Self Comes to Mind: Constructing the Conscious Brain. — New York: Pantheon, 2010.

42. Damasio, A. The Feeling of What Happens: Body and Emotion in the Making of Consciousness. — New York: Harcourt, 1999.

43. Dehaene, S. & Naccache, L. (2001). Towards a Cognitive Neuroscience of Consciousness: Basic Evidence and a Workspace Framework. Cognition, 79, 1–37.

Edelman, G. M. (2004). Wider than the Sky: The Phenomenal Gift of Consciousness. Yale University Press.

Dehaene, S. (2014). Consciousness and the Brain. Viking.

Lobasyuk, B.A. (2015). Setevaya nejrofiziologiya. Odessa: HGEU.

Llinas, R. R. (2001). I of the Vortex: From Neurons to Self. MIT Press.

Steriade, M. (1996). Arousal: Re-Examining the Reticular Activating System. Science, 272, 225–227.

44. Dehaene, S. (2014). Consciousness and the Brain: Deciphering How the Brain Codes Our Thoughts. Penguin.

45. Dehaene, S. Consciousness and the Brain: Deciphering How the Brain Codes Our Thoughts. — New York: Viking, 2014.

46. Dehaene, S., & Changeux, J. P. (2011). Experimental and theoretical approaches to conscious processing. Neuron, 70(2), 200–227.

47. Dehaene, S., Naccache, L. Towards a cognitive neuroscience of consciousness: basic evidence and a workspace framework. Cognition, 2001.

48. Dennett, D. Consciousness Explained. — Boston: Little, Brown, 1991.

49. Edelman, G. M. & Tononi, G. (2000). A Universe of Consciousness: Ho

50. Engel, A. K., & Singer, W. (2001). Temporal binding and the neural correlates of sensory awareness. Trends in Cognitive Sciences, 5(1), 16–25.

51. Epskamp S., Fried E.I. (2018). Psychological network analysis.

52. Epskamp S., Fried E.I. Psychological network analysis. Annual Review of Clinical Psychology, 2018.

53. Freud, S. New Introductory Lectures on Psychoanalysis. — New York: Norton, 1933.

54. Freud, S. The Ego and the Id (1923).

55. Freud, S. The Unconscious (1915) // Standard Edition, Vol. XIV. London: Hogarth Press, 1957.

56. Freud, S. The Unconscious. — London: Hogarth Press, 1915.

57. Fried E.I., et al. (2021). Personality network neuroscience: Promises and challenges on the way toward a unifying framework of individual variability.

Christensen A.P., Golino H.F., Epskamp S. (2023). Architecture and relationships among cognition, mental health and other human domains +revealed by network analysis perspective.

Cramer A.O.J., et al. (2010). Comorbidity: a network perspective.

58. Fried E.I., et al. Personality network neuroscience: Promises and challenges. Network Neuroscience, 2021.

59. Friston, K. (2019). The Free Energy Principle: A Unified Brain Theory? Nature Reviews Neuroscience, 11(2), 127–138.

60. Graziano, M. S. A. (2019). Rethinking Consciousness: A Scientific Theory of Subjective Experience. W.W. Norton.

61. Green, A. The Fabric of Affect in the Psychoanalytic Discourse. — London: Routledge, 2003.

62. Hameroff, S., Penrose, R. (2014). Consciousness in the Universe: A Review of the 'Orch OR' Theory. Physics of Life Reviews, 11(1), 39–78.

63. Kihlstrom, J. F. "The Cognitive Unconscious." Science, 237, 1987, pp. 1445–1452.

64. Kihlstrom, J.F. The Cognitive Unconscious. // Science, 1987, 237, pp. 1445–1452.

65. Koch, C., Massimini, M., Boly, M., & Tononi, G. (2016). Neural correlates of consciousness: progress and problems. Nature Reviews Neuroscience, 17, 307–321.

66. Kossakowski J.J., et al. (2024). A psychological network analysis of the relationship among component importance measures.

67. LeDoux, J. The Emotional Brain. — New York: Simon & Schuster, 1996.

68. Libet, B. Unconscious cerebral initiative and the role of conscious will in voluntary action. Behavioral and Brain Sciences, 1985.

69. Lobasyuk B.A., Zamkova A.V., Bodelan M.I. Network Semantic-Topological Model of Electrogenesis. // Journal of Cognitive and Systems Neuroscience. — 2024. — Vol. 5(2). — P. 55–72.

70. Lobasyuk, B. A. Network Semantic-Topological Model of Electrogenesis. // Psychology and Neuroscience, 2024.

71. Lobasyuk, B. A. Network Semantic-Topological Model of Electrogenesis. // Psychology and Neuroscience, 2024.

72. Lobasyuk, B.A. Network Neurophysiology. — Odesa: HSEU Press, 2023.

73. Lobasyuk, B.A. Network Semantic-Topological Model of Electrogenesis. // Psychology and Neuroscience, 2024.

74. Lobasyuk, B.A., Bodelan, M.I., Zamkova, A.V. Network Semantic-Topological Method in Psychology. — Odesa, 2025.

75. Lobasyuk, B.A., Bodelan, M.I., Zamkova, A.V. Network Semantic-Topological Method in Psychology. — Odesa, 2025.

76. Lobasyuk, B.A., Bodelan, M.I., Zamkova, A.V. Network Semantic-Topological Met

77. Lobasyuk, B.A., Bodelan, M.I., Zamkova, A.V. Setevoj semantiko-topologicheskij metod v psihologii. — Odessa, 2025.

78. Lobasyuk, B.A., Bodelan, M.I., Zamkova, A.V. Setevoj semantiko-topologicheskij metod v psihologii. — Odessa, 2025.

79. Mashour, G. A., Roelfsema, P., Changeux, J.-P., Dehaene, S. (2020). Conscious Processing and the Global Neuronal Workspace Hypothesis. Neuron, 105(5), 776–798.

80. Michell L., et al. Psychological Network Analysis of General Self Efficacy in High vs. Low Resilient Functioning Healthy Adults. Frontiers in Psychiatry, 2021.

81. Nietzsche, F. Jenseits von Gut und Bose. — Leipzig, 1886.

82. Northoff, G., Heinzel, A., de Greck, M., Bermpohl, F., Dobrowolny, H., & Panksepp, J. (2006). Self-referential processing in our brain – a meta-analysis of imaging studies on the self. NeuroImage, 31(1), 440–457.

83. Pajevic S., Plenz D. (2012). Neurocognitive networks: findings, models, and theory.

84. Panksepp, J. (1998). Affective Neuroscience. Oxford University Press.

Plotnik, J. M., de Waal, F. B. M., Reiss, D. (2006). Self-recognition in an Asian Elephant. PNAS, 103, 17053–17057.

85. Panksepp, J. Affective Neuroscience: The Foundations of Human and Animal Emotions. — New York: Oxford Univ. Press, 1998.

86. Premack, D., & Woodruff, G. (1978). Does the chimpanzee have a theory of mind? Behavioral and Brain Sciences, 1(4), 515–526.

87. Pribram K. Languages of the Brain. — Monterey, 1971.

88. Raichle, M. E. et al. A Default Mode of Brain Function // PNAS, 2001. Vol. 98 (2), p. 676–682.

89. Reber, A. Implicit Learning and Tacit Knowledge. — Oxford University Press, 1993.

90. Rosenthal, D. M. (2005). Consciousness and Mind. Oxford University Press.

91. Schopenhauer, A. Die Welt als Wille und Vorstellung. — Leipzig, 1819.

92. Sergent, C., Baillet, S., Dehaene, S. Timing of the brain events underlying access to consciousness during the attentional blink. Nature Neuroscience, 2005.

93. Sergent, C., Baillet, S., Dehaene, S. Timing of the brain events underlying access to consciousness during the attentional blink. Nature Neuroscience, 2005.

94. Seth, A. (2021). Being You: A New Science of Consciousness. Faber & Faber.

95. Seth, A. Being You: A New Science of Consciousness. — London: Faber & Faber, 2021.

96. Shen X., et al. The network and interactive pattern of social adjustment and psychological symptoms in patients with spinal cord injury. BMC Psychology, 2025.

97. Shettleworth, S.J. Cognition, Evolution, and Behavior. — Oxford University Press, 2010.

98. Smith L., et al. (2017). Network Models for Cognitive Development and Intelligence.

Pajevic S., Plenz D. Neurocognitive networks: findings, models, and theory. Trends in Cognitive Sciences, 2012.

99. Smith L., et al. (2017). Network Models for Cognitive Development and Intelligence.

100. Smith L., et al. Network Models for Cognitive Development and Intelligence. Journal of Intelligence, 2017.

101. Smith, J. D., Shields, W. E., Washburn, D. A. (1995). Metacognition in Rhesus Monkeys. Cognition, 77, 23–41.

102. Tononi, G. (2004). An information integration theory of consciousness. BMC Neuroscience, 5, 42.

103. Tononi, G. (2008). Consciousness as Integrated Information: A Provisional Manifesto. Biological Bulletin, 215(3), 216–242.

104. Tononi, G. An Information Integration Theory of Consciousness (2008).

105. Tononi, G. An Information Integration Theory of Consciousness. — BMC Neuroscience, 2008.

106. Tononi, G. An Information Integration Theory of Consciousness. BMC Neuroscience, 2008.

107. Tononi, G., Koch, C. (2015). Consciousness: Here, There and Everywhere? Philosophical Transactions of the Royal Society B, 370(1668)

www.ingramcontent.com/pod-product-compliance
Lightning Source LLC
LaVergne TN
LVHW022109200926
848481LV00003B/1118